23 TRUTHS

THAT TRANSFORM MANAGERS INTO LEADERS

23 TRUTHS

THAT TRANSFORM MANAGERS INTO LEADERS

TOM GEHRING

ISBN 978-1-7327992-6-4 (hardcover)
ISBN 978-1-7327992-7-1 (paperback)
ISBN 978-1-7327992-8-8 (ebook)

Published by Far Peaks Publishing, San Diego, California
www.farpeaksconsulting.com

Copyright © 2022 Tom Gehring. All rights reserved.
No part of this book may be reproduced, stored in a retrieval system, or transmitted by any means, electronic, mechanical, photocopying, recording, or otherwise, without the written permission from the copyright holder.

For ordering information or special discounts for bulk purchases or customized editions, please contact
Far Peaks Publishing, (619) 206-8282

Cover and Interior Design and Composition
by The Book Designers, www.bookdesigners.com

Publishing Consulting by Karla Olson, BookStudio, www.bookstudiobooks.com

Printed in the United States of America

DEDICATION

This book is dedicated to the *spirit* of the
Polynesian mariners of the Pacific.
They crossed vast distances with nothing more than
the stars in the night sky, incredible optimism,
and courage I cannot even fathom.
May we all strive to emulate them.

TABLE OF CONTENTS

Chapter 1 - The Big Picture 1
Chapter 2 - Context for the 23 Truths 5
Chapter 3 - The Organization of the Book 9

SECTION ONE – FOCUSING 11
Chapter 4 - If You Don't Know Where You're Going, Any Road
    Will Get You There 13
Chapter 5 - Make the Main Thing the Main Thing 21
Chapter 6 - What You See Depends on Where You Stand 29

SECTION TWO – LEADING 35
Chapter 7 - The Buck Stops Here 37
Chapter 8 - Lead from the Front 43
Chapter 9 - May the Force Be with You 49

SECTION THREE – ACTIONING 55
Chapter 10 - What Are You Going to Do Differently on
    Monday? 57
Chapter 11 - Plans Are Nothing, Planning Is Everything 63
Chapter 12 - Improvise, Adapt, and Overcome 71
Chapter 13 - It Is Better to Sweat in Peace than Bleed
    in War 77
Chapter 14 - Why? Why? Why? Why? Why? Why? 83

SECTION FOUR – PHILOSOPHIZING 89
Chapter 15 - Do What You Can, With What You've Got, Where
    You Are At 91
Chapter 16 - Nothing Hard Is Ever Easy 97
Chapter 17 - What's the Right Thing to Do Here? 101
Chapter 18 - Life Is Tough, but It's Tougher If You're
    Not Smart 109

Chapter 19 - KISS 115
Chapter 20 - Perpetual Optimism Is a Force Multiplier 117
Chapter 21 - Everything Is Connected to Everything Else 121

SECTION FIVE – LEARNING 127
Chapter 22 - Those Who Do Not Learn from History
              Are Doomed to Repeat It 129
Chapter 23 - Make Mistakes. Learn from Them. Move On 133
Chapter 24 - Listen 137

SECTION SIX – CARING 143
Chapter 25 - Leaders Eat Last 145
Chapter 26 - Life Is Short, Eat Dessert First! 149

SECTION SEVEN – CASE STUDIES 155
Chapter 27 - Case Study #1 – Little Cog in a Big Wheel 157
Chapter 28 - Case Study #2 – Big Cog in a Little Wheel 165
Chapter 29 - Case Study #3 – Janus 173

Summary and Afterword 181
Acknowledgments 183
About the Author 185
Bibliography 187
Appendix 1 – 23 Truths 188
Appendix 2 – The keys to transformation for all 23 truths 191
Appendix 3 – What are you going to do differently
              on Monday for all 23 truths 197
Appendix 4 – One CEO's Philosophy Statement – Pretty
              Good Rules to Live By 203
Index 207

PREFACE

Why did I write this book? Because I believe teaching the next generation—and teaching them well—is one of the most important things humans do.

For most of us, our careers progress linearly from apprentice worker to expert doer, then to novice manager, then to expert manager, then to novice leader, and finally, to expert leader.

If you've picked up this book, you are likely on a journey toward leadership.

But *how* do you make the transition from manager to leader? Improvisation? Trial and error? Absorption? Winging it?

After much reflection, I realized a need for an illuminated path to *transform managers into leaders*. So I chose 23 of my favorite wisdoms[1] to shed light on that transformational journey.

The ancient Polynesian mariners crossed vast stretches of the Pacific by referring to the stars in the night sky. For example, using Arcturus as a zenith star,[2] they could find Hawaii in an empty ocean. That knowledge of celestial navigation was passed down from one generation to the next for millennia.

I hope that these 23 truths will guide your journey, just like the twinkling lights from distant stars helped the ancient mariners find dots of land in a desolate ocean.

It has been a joy to reflect on my past and to help my readers with their future. Godspeed and good luck.

—*Tom Gehring*
San Diego, February 2022

---

[1] I appreciate that the grammarians will not like my pluralization of *wisdom* into *wisdoms*.... It's not the first of my neologisms!

[2] A zenith star is one that rises above the horizon on the same bearing as your destination—if you follow an island's zenith star, eventually you reach that island.

The Big Picture

Doing-Managing-Leading-Teaching

I believe there are four stages in the professional trajectories for most talented individuals:

- <u>Doing</u> can range from the elementary (rote assembly-line work) to the incredibly complex (brain surgery). It involves accomplishing a specific, clearly delineated task. Mastering a task can take from minutes of training to decades of learning.
- <u>Managing</u> is getting something done that would not have occurred without you.[3] It is causing *others* to accomplish tasks. Think of management as the plural of doing.
- <u>Leading</u> is taking a group of people to a place where they would not have gotten to without you.[4] That "place" can be anything from a geographic location to an entirely new organization. Without the leader, the followers would not have reached that "place," no matter how hardworking and brilliant.

---

3 *11 Questions Great Managers Ask & Answer*, my second book
4 *7 Roles Great Leaders Don't Delegate*, my first book

- <u>Teaching</u> is sharing your hard-earned knowledge about doing, managing, and leading with others. Using a sports metaphor, it's when you go from playing on the frontlines to coaching on the sidelines. It's when you go from leader to elder.[5]

Transitioning

Almost all of us have something we are good at doing, usually preceded or accompanied by significant training or education. For example, my wife is a physician, and I trained as an electrical engineer.

Sooner or later, most of us grow beyond a specific skill to management and/or leadership.

You do not have to become a manager. Many doers are not, and never want to be, managers.

You do not have to have experience as a manager to be a leader. Many great leaders are not managers.

You do not have to become a leader. Many managers are not, and never want to be, leaders.

But the most effective of those who have transcended doing are both leaders and managers. Most have become great managers first and then great leaders.

The purpose of this book is to help managers transform themselves into leaders by listing and discussing powerful, time-tested ideas encapsulated in simple, easy-to-remember, and catchy sayings.

Organizing the 23 Truths

The longer I looked at the 23 truths, the more I realized that these wise sayings could be categorized into six broad themes. So I used a single word, an action verb, to describe the six categories of wisdoms that will help you transition from doer to manager to leader.

---

[5] It's the stage I find myself in, and the reason I wrote this and my previous two books.

Focusing

Leaders must have a much broader perspective than managers, but since they have a wider field of view, they also have to selectively focus more than managers. I found these three aphorisms most useful to help me focus as I transitioned from doer to manager to leader:

- ✓ If you don't know where you're going, any road will get you there.
- ✓ Make the main thing the main thing.
- ✓ What you see depends on where you stand.

Leading

There are thousands of books and ideas that describe leadership. These three simple, easy-to-remember sayings have helped me define my leadership style and helped me make the transition from doer to manager to leader:

- ✓ The buck stops here.
- ✓ Lead from the front.
- ✓ May the force be with you.

Actioning

As managers transition to leaders, they have to learn a more proactive approach to taking action. These five time-tested maxims helped me formulate my actions as I transitioned from doer to manager to leader.

- ✓ What are you going to do differently on Monday?
- ✓ Improvise, adapt, and overcome.
- ✓ Plans are nothing. Planning is everything.
- ✓ It is better to sweat in peace than bleed in war.
- ✓ Why? Why? Why? Why? Why?

Philosophizing

Leaders need a philosophical basis for how they think. These seven wise thoughts, passed down for generations, are what helped me keep my head straight as I transitioned from doer to manager to leader:

- ✓ Do what you can, with what you have, where you are at.
- ✓ Nothing hard is ever easy.
- ✓ What's the right thing to do here?
- ✓ Life is tough, but it's tougher if you're not smart.
- ✓ KISS—keep it simple & short.
- ✓ Perpetual optimism is a force multiplier.
- ✓ Everything is connected to everything else.

Learning

Transitioning yourself from doer to manager to leader requires active learning. These three precepts were most helpful:

- ✓ Those who do not learn from history are doomed to repeat it.
- ✓ Make mistakes. Learn from them. Move on.
- ✓ Listen.

Caring

Finally, the farther up the doing-managing-leading continuum you move, the more you must care for your team and, more importantly, yourself. These two maxims embodied what matters most about caring:

- ✓ Leaders eat last.
- ✓ Life is short, eat dessert first.

And there you have the big picture: 23 great ideas grouped into six categories that light the way for anyone transitioning from doing to managing to leading.

Context for the 23 Truths

Why do you call them "truths"?
There are a number of labels that could define the 23:
- ✓ aphorisms, described as "a pithy observation that contains a general truth," or
- ✓ wisdoms, a grammatically incorrect neologism that pluralizes wisdom, or
- ✓ maxims, or
- ✓ precepts, or
- ✓ sayings, or
- ✓ truths.

While all six labels are essentially interchangeable, I settled on "truths" as the easiest to understand, least grammatically offensive, and most in touch with the fundamental nature of the 23.

What are the characteristics of these phrases?
Whatever we call them, the 23 all share several characteristics:
- ✓ they are short,
- ✓ they are catchy,
- ✓ they are easy to remember,
- ✓ they capture an essential leadership idea.

In many cases, they have famous authors.

In several cases, they have been attributed to multiple originators.

Why 23?
When I first jotted down the ideas that would become this book, there were 23 sayings that I liked and used, and frequently repeated out loud.

From the thousands of leadership sayings, wisdoms, truths, maxims, and aphorisms, I had picked the 23 that were most relevant to my journey from doing to managing to leading.

> **The 23 truths are the DNA for your transition from doer to manager to leader**

There was nothing magical about my choice of the ninth prime number. It seemed like a nice balance of not enough and not too much.

But after choosing to limit my universe of truths to 23, the DNA metaphor struck me. There are 23 chromosomes in the human DNA[6]—so think of the 23 truths as the DNA for your transition from doer to manager to leader.

---

6 For those like me who bailed on Biology 101 in college, the 23 strands of deoxyribonucleic acid (DNA), coiled in the iconic double-helix, carry the genetic instructions for the development, functioning, growth, and reproduction of all known organisms and many viruses. It is literally the blueprint for life.

A final word before we start

These are absolutely not the only 23 truths, wisdoms, maxims, aphorisms, or sayings that will help you transform yourself into a leader.

I encourage you to add to or subtract from these 23. But create for yourself a menu of wisdoms—the stars you steer by—for the daily work of leadership.

The Organization of the Book

Organization of the book

In sections one through six, I explain the transformational truths. The 23 chapters, organized in six sections, present and discuss one of the transformational truths.

Section seven presents three case studies describing fictional journeys toward leadership and how the 23 truths facilitated that transformation to leadership.

Appendix one lists all 23 truths on one place for easy reproduction.

Appendix two lists, in one convenient place, all the key transformational points.

Appendix three lists, in one convenient place, all the things to do differently on Monday.

Appendix four is a verbatim copy of my CEO's Philosophy Statement.[7]

---

[7] As CEO, I collected a number of ideas and sayings that became my operating philosophy. I hung a copy in my office, inches from my head, for two reasons. Obviously, it served as a reminder to me of what I believed. Not so obviously, and more importantly, it gave permission for my team to come in and point out, literally, how something *I* was doing was not in consonance with I said I expected *them* to do.

Summarizing the transition

In chapter 5, I argue that critical to focusing is keeping the main thing the main thing.

The main thing for this book is lighting a path for a transition from management to leadership.

At the end of each chapter, I include a list of the actions a manager can and should take to speed their transformation to leader. That is the main thing for this book!

Ideas to action

You start with ideas—but eventually, sooner rather than later, if your idea is to have impact, you have to translate any idea into action.

I'm fond of asking students in a leadership course I teach, "Okay, so what are you going to do differently on Monday?" In fact, that's one of the 23 truths.

At the end of each chapter, I present ideas on how you can operationalize the chapter's concepts under the heading "What are you going to do differently on Monday?"

Chapter lengths

"Cut to the chase" is one of my favorite sayings, even at home! I'm not patient.

Some chapters are short because I want to give the content stand-alone recognition—but without excessive repetition.

The case studies

There are three case studies in section seven:
- ✓ #1—Sasha is transitioning from manager to leader.
- ✓ #2—Margaret is transitioning from doer to manager and leader.
- ✓ #3—Jorge is transitioning straight from doer to leader.

SECTION 1

FOCUSING

This section is about consciously deciding your focus.

Focus is both a noun and a verb.

✓ You must *act to focus,* and

✓ You must know *what to focus on.*

To transform yourself into a leader, I suggest you keep the following three maxims close at hand. They all speak to what you, as the leader, should be looking at.

- *If you don't know where you're going, any road will get you there.* You have to have a vision.

- *Make the main thing the main thing.* You have to decide what matters most.
- *What you see depends on where you stand.* You have to make your perspective—that which you are specifically looking at—a conscious decision.

If You Don't Know Where You're Going, Any Road Will Get You There

Origin

"If you don't know where you're going, any road will get you there" is a paraphrase of an exchange between Alice and the Cheshire Cat in Lewis Carroll's *Alice's Adventures in Wonderland.*

> "Would you tell me, please, which way I ought to go from here?"
> "That depends a good deal on where you want to get to," said the Cat.
> "I don't much care where—" said Alice.
> "Then it doesn't matter which way you go," said the Cat.
> "—so long as I get SOMEWHERE," Alice added as an explanation.
> "Oh, you're sure to do that," said the Cat, "if you only walk long enough."

23 TRUTHS THAT TRANSFORM MANAGERS INTO LEADERS

The concept

"Where the heck are we headed?" is probably the *second* strategic question any leader should ask.[8]

Yet, the examples of organizations or individuals not having a strategic direction—a strategic vision—are legion.

And the real-world impacts of vision-free organizations or individuals are almost universally unpleasant.

That's why this is the *first* of the 23 truths: you must start with clarity about where you are going.

From managerial pathways to leadership outcomes

A vacation analogy is helpful (and a lot more fun than this boring work stuff).

When the family gathers to figure out the next big trip, there are three fundamental questions to be answered:

- ✓ Where are we starting from? Usually, but not always, home.
- ✓ Where are we going? Closely related, and sometimes in the same breath, is the "why" question. Why are we going *there*? Usually, this is the crux of the matter.
- ✓ How will we get there and back? There are many complex logistics issues associated with a trip. Usually, this is where families (or the designated organizer) spend most of their time and energy.

> **Where are we starting from?**
> **Where are we going?**
> **How will we get there and back?**

Most managers are quite sensitive to those three questions. They *really* do want to identify a starting point, an endpoint, and a pathway.

---

[8] The first question is, simplified, "What's going on here?" See chapter 4 of *7 Roles Great Leaders Don't Delegate,* where I describe the first of seven non-delegatable roles of the leader as that of *sensing*—determining the state of the organizational or personal universe.

However, the focus of most managers is usually on executing the pathway—either implementing the strategies or the work plan.[9]

Managers are focused on getting stuff done.[10]

Leaders focus on outcomes, endpoints, or destinations.

The transformation from manager to leader revolves around changing the manager's focus from dutifully executing the pathway (strategies or work plans) to thinking deeply about the start points and endpoints of the organizational journey.

How do leaders focus themselves and their organizations?

Deciding your future is usually referred to as strategic planning. There have been volumes written about strategic planning and visioning. So let's keep it simple. You need to identify three things, just like in the vacation analogy:

- ✓ Where is your organization—the present tense.
- ✓ Where does your organization want to go—your destination—the future tense—the vision.
- ✓ The path your organization will use to get from here to there—the strategies or the work plan.

Changing how you think about the present

Leaders spend an enormous amount of up-front time making sure they clearly understand the environment (the present tense) where their organization and their people are really at.

Is your assessment of the environment (the present tense) really accurate? Have you factored in all the information sources? Have you looked wide and deep? Have you questioned the assumptions about the current environment? There are so many questions to ask.

---

9   Strategies are usually few in number but global or overarching. The strategies are applicable to the entire organization. Work plans are quite specific and usually short-term, and applicable to some subset of the organization.
10 Realistically, *someone* has to be focused on getting it done.

As managers transform into leaders, they do not blindly accept the current assessment of the present tense. On the contrary, developing leaders spend more and more time improving and refining their understanding of the present tense.

Back to going on vacation. Before you decide where to go on vacation, you have to know from where you are starting. Home? Your in-laws' house? Your 50th high school reunion? Do you understand your resources? How much time do you have? How much money do you have, and how much are you willing to spend? What are the interests of your spouse? The kids?

The questions are nearly endless, but the point is singular: know your present. Because if your understanding of the present is flawed, your journey is likely doomed. | **Know your present**

Changing how you think about the future

Next, leaders spend so much more of their valuable time than managers working on a vision of a desirable future state. This requires a significant amount of the leader's and their direct reports' time and mental energy.

Visualize your future | The vacation analogy continues. Are we going skiing or snorkeling? Is this a romantic getaway for two or a mad scramble with kids and friends in tow? I love snorkeling, but he wants to go skiing? She wants to go to Europe, but I would love to go to New Zealand?

What's our destination, and what are our goals?

Visualize your future.

Changing your thinking about how you are going to get there

The good news is that most, but regretfully not all, managers are very good at the details of how to get from here to there.

So how does the manager transform themselves into a leader? They delegate effectively.

Back to our vacation analogy. Your spouse is a superlative logistician. Let that person make the airline and lodging reservations. Your kids love wave boarding. Let them figure out the best location and rental shop on the web.

Effective leadership is all about effective delegation *once* you decide the start and endpoints.

How are you going to shift focus?
It is unrealistic for a manager to simply stop thinking about executing the strategies and work plans.

But in the simplest terms, managers who want to become leaders need to think more strategically and less tactically.

So what can a manager wanting to be a leader do?
- ✓ Talk with their boss(es) about the organizational direction.
- ✓ Think about the organizational direction for the work unit they are directly responsible for.
- ✓ Adopt a more strategic and less tactical mindset.

What's our next move?
When my bride asked me to help a philanthropic organization from our church—let's call them "Wings for Peace" (WFP)—my correct answer was, "Of course, dear!"

At her request, I met with the founders of WFP and asked them, "Where do you want WFP to be at some point in the future, say 18 months?"

I heard a lot of great short-term stuff: create a website, have some events, raise money, get more members on board, and host a fundraiser (all totally appropriate but completely disconnected tasks).

But I continued, "What's your vision for WFP; where do you want WFP to be at some point in the future? What are your strategies to get there?"

Silence.

As you transform from manager to leader, two essential and fundamental distinctions must be clearly understood. Tasks are not strategies, and strategies do not make a vision. Rather, a vision creates strategies that generate tasks.

WFP had a clear picture of the problem they were trying to address, the resources at their disposal, and their current efforts. They knew their present.

But their future was diffuse. Asked the same question, "Where are we going?" the founders all had different answers.

The first task was to brainstorm a vision for WFP. Visions are statements of a desirable and achievable future state, and entail either an explicit or implicit time horizon.

So we convened an offsite to articulate a WFP vision and agreed that the time horizon was three years.

Then, and only then, did we create four strategies to help WFP achieve said vision in the next three years.

Then, and only then, did we create multi-page task lists to achieve the strategies.

Vision to strategies to tasks.

But if you don't know where you're going, any road will take you there.

KEYS TO THE TRANSFORMATION

As managers transform themselves into leaders, they:
- Shift from dutifully executing the pathway (strategies or work plans) to thinking deeply about the start points and endpoints of the organizational journey.
- Do not blindly accept the current assessment of the present.
- Spend more and more time improving and refining their understanding of the present tense.
- Think more strategically and less tactically.
- Distinguish between tasks and strategies.
- Recognize that strategies do not a vision make.

WHAT AM I GOING TO DO DIFFERENTLY ON MONDAY TO TRANSFORM MYSELF FROM A MANAGER INTO A LEADER?

- Schedule a formal review of the current environment, vision, and strategies.
- Ask to see the work plan and the strategic plan, and:
    - ✓ Check that the work plan is detailed and site-specific.
    - ✓ Check that the strategic plan is high-level and applicable to everyone.
- Ask to see the metrics associated with the work plan, the strategic plan, and the outcomes associated with the vision.

Make the Main Thing the Main Thing

Origin

While many have articulated the concept, Stephen Covey, in his seminal book, *The 7 Habits of Highly Effective People,* popularized it and made it explicit.

The concept

This truth is almost laughably simple—spend your finite time and energy on what *really* matters and de-focus from what doesn't *really* matter.

> **Spend your finite time and energy on what *really* matters**

It's all about priorities.

OK, that's so obvious—we're done here—go directly to the next chapter!

Well, not so fast...

Prioritizing the priorities

The transformation from manager to leader revolves around changing the manager's focus from treating most everything with roughly equal priority to explicitly making one thing a higher priority than everything else.

In the eponymous daily cartoon strip *Dilbert* which highlights the darkly humorous challenges of life in the cubicle, Dilbert's boss drives his team absolutely nuts by insisting on multiple #1 priorities. I didn't know whether to laugh or cry; you just cannot have multiple #1s.

The problems with implementing the concept

Making the main thing the main thing is so much easier said than done. That means aggressive prioritization. That means disappointing some (or many).

You will likely get pushback from your team.
- ✓ Your team will disagree with your "main thing" and insist that you make *their* particular focus the *real* "main thing."
- ✓ Your teammates will confuse, deliberately or inadvertently, that if it's not *the* "main thing," it won't get done. In the vernacular, you have to be able to walk and chew gum at the same time!
- ✓ Your fellow managers will not be enthusiastic when their "main thing" isn't the organizational "main thing."

But it's more complex than simply dealing with pushback from your fellow team members.

There are three structural problems associated with making the main thing the main thing.
- ✓ Too many "main things."
- ✓ Too many roles, each of which has multiple "main things."
- ✓ Overwhelming distractions.

We are greedy

The first problem with implementing this idea is that many of us do not have a clearly articulated "main thing" in our professional or personal roles. We are greedy—we want to accomplish a lot—so rather than prune ruthlessly down to *one* "main thing," we kid ourselves into thinking we can achieve *many* "main things."

> We kid ourselves into thinking we can achieve *many* "main things"

There is a critical distinction between accomplishing a lot of "main things" and accomplishing a lot of things. Most of us get a lot done; if you are reading this, you are likely organized and can balance multiple projects. But you cannot accomplish a lot of "main things."

> Managers try to do it all
> Leaders pick the most important and ruthlessly prioritize

Managers try to do it all.

Leaders pick the most important and ruthlessly prioritize.

We have no priorities

The flipside to having too many priorities is having none at all. You cannot avoid prioritizing!

We have too many roles

To make matters even more complicated, we have multiple roles—leader, manager, parent, volunteer, spouse—and each of those roles has at least one "main thing."

In my teacher/mentor role, my "main thing" in 2020 was to write the first draft of this book. I knew I needed three or so distraction-free weeks. No way was that going to happen at home (the disruptions, the tasks, the phone calls, the chores, etc...).[11] So, four months before starting to write, I carved three weeks out of my schedule and reserved our distraction-free vacation home in the Sierras, 400 miles from distraction central in San Diego.

---

11   Regretfully and ironically, most of the distractions were self-inflicted!

I made writing the first draft of this book my "main thing" in my teacher/mentor role and prioritized my valuable time accordingly.

Managers, to transform into leaders, have to clearly understand and differentiate their multiple roles, and then assign a "main thing" for each role.

Sometimes, you gotta make a really hard choice...
One of the conundrums of modern life is that we have many roles, each with at least one main thing. Sometimes we can harmoniously follow multiple main things—and sometimes not. Choosing the primacy of your main thing can be achingly hard.

A personal example. I had served at sea for over a dozen years with the ultimate goal of command of a nuclear submarine, my main thing. I was on the fast track. When it came time to go to my second-in-command job, the Navy wanted me to move to Washington (state) to serve as XO[12] on a ballistic missile submarine. It was "career-enhancing," the next step on the ladder. It was also made very clear that not going to Washington would take my career off the fast track.

But I also had a partner, my wife Cathy, a practicing psychiatrist. Unlike other specialties, psychiatry is very dependent on stable relationships with fellow (referring) physicians and long-term relationships with their patients.

If I moved, she could not.

I had two "main things" in direct conflict. I had to choose between career and family.

I picked family and stayed in San Diego.[13]

---

12 XO is the abbreviation for Executive Officer, the second in command on Navy ships.
13 It's funny how life works out: I wound up not going to full-time command, but had two exceptionally fulfilling Navy jobs before retirement, was able to see the birth of my son and participate in his first years (which would never have happened in command at sea), and found a path to very meaningful second and third careers. And we're still married after 38 years.

There are too many shiny objects

Today's world does not make focusing easy. The computer's siren song,[14] the nagging emails, and the cell phone all beg for attention. The distractions are many, and the time is limited.

As you transform yourself from manager to leader, you must learn to ruthlessly ignore the distractions. For some fraction of your day, turn off the computer, put the cell phone in another room, and close the door (literally or figuratively). Learn to say "no."

As I was writing the second draft, I discovered a room in our house that did not have WiFi. I could have easily installed a repeater but quickly came to treasure the quiet. I learned to appreciate the unobstructed sunrise view over the mountains in the distance. That room became my distraction-free zone! What's yours?

Yes, you can (and must) have multiple "main things"

Wait, I just said you should have a (singular) "main thing." So, no, I'm not talking out of both sides of my mouth!

For each of your roles, you need one "main thing." But since you have multiple roles, it stands to reason that you will have multiple "main things."

I have several roles: spouse, parent, teacher/mentor, program director, and community member. In each role, I have one "main thing," as well as lots and lots and lots of tasks.

> **Every role has one main thing**

But it's the five role-specific "main things" that lay first claim to my time and attention.

---

14 In Homer's *Odyssey*, he wrote of the Sirens, whose beautiful singing lured countless sailors to shipwreck on the rocky island of Anthemoessa. Odysseus knew that he must pass the Sirens to get to his homeland, so he took action to protect the lives of his sailors and himself. He tied himself to the mast and gave his sailors earplugs.

Focus

You have to decide what one thing tops everything else for each of your roles.

I recommend you commit yourself to writing down and posting your "main thing" in a prominent place, perhaps even making it your "pop-up" on your computer and cell phone.

Then frequently ask yourself, "Am I focused on my 'main thing'?"

I was the XO, equivalent to being Chief Operating Officer (COO), on a very large Navy ship, the submarine tender *USS McKee (AS-41)*. As with all vessels, *McKee* required periodic dry-docking and attendant maintenance.

We, in senior leadership, identified that *McKee* and her crew's "main thing" was to "complete the maintenance period safely and on time."

Everything we did was directly connected to that simple premise. Captain Tom Etter, my skipper, repeatedly voiced (almost to the point of eye-rolling among his officers) that we make the "main thing the main thing." So we plastered a copy of the "main thing" everywhere. We announced it every morning. We made it part of every day. We assigned the main thing first priority on our time and attention. And we accomplished that "main thing."

Thousands of routine tasks still had to be accomplished. For example, my yeomen needed to produce personnel reports, the cooks had to make meals, the shore patrol had to keep order, and the list went on and on. But everything took second place to something associated with safely completing the maintenance period on time. So, for example, half of the yeomen were assigned as bus drivers for our shuttles from our secure parking lot, which ensured the crew was safe on their way to and from work in a sketchy neighborhood.

Learn to shift priorities

Priorities change. As managers transform into leaders, they become more adept at shifting priorities.

When I was the Weapons Officer on my second submarine, *USS Haddo* (*SSN 604*), I had trouble with this concept.

I was responsible for loading and offloading torpedoes: 19-foot monsters weighing nearly two tons with lots of explosives. We had to very, very carefully get the torpedo from the pier to the torpedo room through a narrow opening in the ship. Not a good place to have a distracted, bad day!

When we were moving weapons, doing that safely was the "main thing" for the *entire* ship; *nothing* took priority over a safe weapons move. However, as soon as that evolution was completed, a different "main thing" (perhaps a reactor startup or a food load) took precedence.

Back then, as a manager, I could not adapt to the rapidly shifting priorities; I wanted my stuff to be the "main thing" all the time. However, with its rapidly shifting priorities and multiple main things, the real world soon disabused me of that notion!

The intent of this maxim is not to stop all work except that associated with the "main thing." It is simply to prioritize limited assets toward that "main thing." Common sense is authorized!

To transform into leaders, managers must accept and deal with shifting priorities that result in changes in the "main thing."

KEYS TO THE TRANSFORMATION

As managers transform themselves into leaders, they:
- Get away from trying to do it all.
- Pick the most important—the "main thing"—and ruthlessly prioritize it.
- Understand and differentiate multiple roles, and assign a "main thing" to each role.
- Accept and deal with shifting priorities that result in changes to the "main thing."

WHAT AM I GOING TO DO DIFFERENTLY ON MONDAY TO TRANSFORM MYSELF FROM A MANAGER INTO A LEADER?

- Write down the "main thing" for each of your roles.
- Write down the "main thing" for each of your organizations.
- Create a written plan to reduce your distractions at work and at home.
- Schedule a formal review of priorities, including feedback on whether the "main thing" has enough resources.

What You See Depends on Where You Stand

Origin

C.S. Lewis, in *The Magician's Nephew*, wrote, "What you see and what you hear depends a great deal on where you are standing."

The saying has also been attributed to Albert Einstein speaking about his theory of relativity.

The concept

Like the first two truths, this maxim is about focus.

If you are in charge of something, either as a manager or a leader, several things are true:

- ✓ You likely have more experience, wisdom, and perhaps technical skill than many on your team.[15]
- ✓ People pay attention to what *you* are looking at. "What interests my boss fascinates me" is very applicable here.

Sometimes "where you stand" is interpreted as a physical position. Sometimes it is interpreted as a conceptual position—your framing of an issue.

---

15 And if you don't have experience, wisdom, and/or technical skill, you will definitely learn something if you position yourself correctly.

Physical positioning

Almost all nuclear power plants have a set of valves, called primary reliefs, designed to reduce pressure in the reactor plant in the highly unlikely case that fluid pressure increases beyond the normal band. To make sure that the relief valves work correctly, if you ever *really* need them, nuclear power plants test them every so many years. When we performed this test, I was the Engineer Officer of my third submarine, USS *Pogy* (*SSN 647*).

During the test, I had many places I could physically position myself (including in my office)[16]; it was my choice. I chose to stand directly behind the individual recording the high-accuracy pressure gauge that was the arbiter of the pressure at which the valves lifted and reseated. Why? For several reasons:

- ✓ If the relief valve lifted too high or too low, significant and complicated maintenance was required. I wanted to make sure that no one questioned the reading. My positioning was political!
- ✓ I wanted the most experienced set of eyes on the gauge—mine—as a backup. This was a case of "if you blinked, you missed it," and I didn't want to do the test again. My positioning was technical!

Let's say you are the CEO of a not-for-profit, and you're holding your annual gala to raise funds. Where to

What you see is a function of where you *choose* to stand and sit!

stand (or sit)? I would want to sit during dinner with the two biggest donor couples on my left and right. After dinner, I would want to move about to schmooze with as many people as possible. And at the start of cocktail hour, I would want to stand back

---

16 My "office" consisted of a three-person phone booth with about 3 feet by 5 feet of floor space, three bunks, and two fold-down desks. Not exactly palatial, but home sweet home for over three years!

far enough to see that everything was going per plan. During the cocktail hour, I would be chatting up the guests but constantly looking around.

The point of this example is that your positioning is a conscious decision. What you see is a function of where you *choose* to stand and sit!

Conceptual positioning

What you see is also a function of how you position yourself mentally.

Let's say you're the CEO of a small company, and you have a big relocation decision coming up. Your landlord will not renew the lease on your 20,000-square-foot downtown office complex.

If you are only willing to entertain a lease, that's all your realtor will pitch you.

If you are only willing to entertain another downtown office, that's all your realtor will show you.

If, on the other hand, you open your intellectual perspective to consider both a downtown and a suburban location, you will be shown more options.

And if you entertain the whole county as a possibility, you'll be shown a lot more options.

Mental positioning is just as important (often more so) as physical positioning!

> **The difference between a manager and a leader is the scope and depth of their perspective**

As they transform into leaders, managers become much more conscious of their physical and intellectual positioning.

Perspective—three metaphors

Another difference between a manager and a leader is the scope and depth of their perspective.

It's often said of some people that they cannot see the forest for the trees. Following along on this arboreal metaphor, a good manager looks at trees.

A leader, however, looks at the forest.

And *when required*, the leader looks at some trees, and in rare cases, some leaves on some trees—because certain specific details may be crucial to the enterprise!

Kevin Sharer, the retired CEO of biotech giant Amgen, talked about altitude, as a metaphor, in an interview with *Harvard Business Review*.

> ...[a leader] must always be switching between what I call different altitudes—tasks of different levels of abstraction and specificity. At the highest altitude, you're asking the big questions: What are the company's mission and strategy?... At the lowest altitude, you're looking at on-the-ground operations: Did we make that sale? What was the yield on the last lot in that factory? How many days of inventory do we have for a particular drug?
>
> And then there's everything in between.[17]

Another helpful metaphor is that of a zoom lens. A manager will zoom in on a particular scene. A leader will *both* zoom out on the big picture and then zoom in on the details, where appropriate.

Pay attention, very careful attention, to where you stand or sit, and what you are looking at!

> **A manager will zoom in on a particular scene. A leader will *both* zoom out on the big picture and then zoom in on the details**

---

[17] "A Time for Growth: An Interview with Amgen CEO Kevin Sharer," by Paul Hemp, from *HBR*, July–August 2004

KEYS TO THE TRANSFORMATION

As managers transform themselves into leaders, they:
- Become much more deliberate about their physical or intellectual positioning.
- Deliberately expand the scope of their thinking by considering many more perspectives and options.
- Become more flexible on the level of detail they examine.
- Ignore neither the big picture nor the details, but learn to zoom from one to the other and everything in between.

WHAT AM I GOING TO DO DIFFERENTLY ON MONDAY TO TRANSFORM MYSELF FROM A MANAGER INTO A LEADER?

- Examine the frame for one major upcoming decision, and assess whether you are looking at the decision too narrowly (or too broadly).
- Develop a list of new or different locations you will look at in the following months.

SECTION 2

LEADING

In general, managers are followers, and leaders are, well, leaders.

That is not to say that managers don't provide specific directions to accomplish a task. But that's direction, not leadership.

I suggest you use three aphorisms to help you transform from manager to leader:

The buck stops here. You have to embrace responsibility.

Lead from the front. Your team expects leadership, not followership.

May the force be with you. Finally, you have to understand and use (but not abuse) your powers.

The Buck Stops Here

Origin

The concept of the boss having the ultimate responsibility is as old as the hills.

The iconic photo of President Harry Truman and the "The Buck Stops Here" plaque on his desk is the usual sourcing of the maxim.

The phrase's etymology is interesting: "Passing the buck" originated from a ritual practiced during card games in the 19th century. Players would place a marker, called a "buck," in front of the dealer. That marker was passed to the next player, along with the responsibility of dealing. Eventually, "passing the buck" became synonymous with passing on responsibility.

The concept

If you're in charge, you have (almost) all the power and all the responsibility. The two go hand in hand.[18]

Ingrained in every naval officer from their time as a midshipman is the ironclad concept that the Captain has total

---

18 If you have all the responsibility, but are limited in power, find something else to do—it's a situation designed to fail.

23 TRUTHS THAT TRANSFORM MANAGERS INTO LEADERS

responsibility—and near-total authority. There are no excuses; if it's their ship, they own it. All of it. No exceptions.

You can dodge some responsibility as a manager. After all, you're just a cog in the wheel. However, as a leader, ducking responsibility is not an option.

The concept of total responsibility can be frightening.

If one of your sailors does something insanely stupid, your fault? Yup.

If one of your employees does something incredibly foolish, your fault? Yup.

"But wait a minute, it was insanely stupid behavior on *their* part. Why is that *my* fault?" wails the novice or the unsuited manager.

The answer is really quite simple:

✓ Why did you not put safeguards into place to prevent something insanely stupid?
✓ Why did you hire people who could do something insanely stupid?
✓ Why did you not train your staff to prevent insanely foolish stuff from happening?
✓ Why did you tolerate (or foster) a climate that allowed something so foolish?

The list goes on, but the concept remains the same: If you're in charge, you own it. All of it. Everything!

If you're in charge, you own it. All of it. Everything!

Excuses
Making excuses is the domain of the weak. Enough said.

Safeguards
Think deeply about what could possibly go wrong and put up barriers to failure.

Think deeply about what needs to go right and implement changes to make it so.

Understanding the root cause(s)
Getting to the bottom of a problem and understanding the root causes of a pain point is the domain of the strong.[19] Enough said.

Embracing responsibility
Managers (maybe) accept responsibility. Leaders embrace responsibility.

> **Managers (maybe) accept responsibility. Leaders embrace responsibility**

My choice of the word "embracing" is very deliberate. Early in my thinking, I used the phrase "accepting responsibility." Accepting responsibility is passive. Embracing responsibility is active. That's a huge difference in behavior.

The transformation from taking responsibility to embracing responsibility is simple in concept and challenging in execution.

If you embrace responsibility, you are proactive. You go looking for ways to excel and go looking for ways to avoid pitfalls.

As a manager transforms into a leader, that person first stops shying away from responsibility, then accepts it, and finally, embraces it.

Who gets the credit?
So, if the leader gets the blame, then who gets the credit?

As managers transform themselves into leaders, they are more and more generous with the plaudits.

Presidents Harry Truman and Ronald Reagan were both often paraphrased as having said, "It's amazing what you get done when you don't care who gets the credit."

---

19 See chapter 14 for a discussion of how to get to the bottom of a problem's cause(s) (I refer to it as "bedrock causality").

Leaders accept blame and give credit to their team. Managers (sometimes) take credit and (often) avoid accountability.

The buck stops on your desk!

KEYS TO THE TRANSFORMATION

As managers transform themselves into leaders, they:
- Stop making excuses.
- Get to the bottom of problems, and understand the root cause(s).
- Stop shying away from responsibility, then accept responsibility, and finally, embrace responsibility.
- Think deeply about what could possibly go wrong and put up barriers to failure.
- Think deeply about what needs to go right and implement changes to make it so.
- When things go well, give credit to their team.
- When things go badly, accept the blame.

WHAT AM I GOING TO DO DIFFERENTLY ON MONDAY TO TRANSFORM MYSELF FROM A MANAGER INTO A LEADER?

- Identify several recent failures and do a deep dive on causality.
- Put a sign on your desk that the buck stops here.
- Pick one current project where you can spread credit.
- For one future project, task your team to proactively search for potential problems.

Lead from the Front

Origin

This is the oldest of the 23 truths. Since our cavemen days, humans have expected their leaders to be in front of the formation, not loitering in the rear.

The concept

Even into the 18th century, British sovereigns led their troops in battle.[20] During World War II, my father served as an officer in the elite mountain troops. He taught me that officers led from the front (literally).

While the origin is military, the applicability of "leading from the front" goes far beyond heading a cavalry charge.

Leading from the front means you don't ask your team to do stuff you would not do.

Leading from the front means you lead by example.

---

[20] On June 27, 1743, King George II personally commanded the British Army against the French at Dettingen.

23 TRUTHS THAT TRANSFORM MANAGERS INTO LEADERS

You accept risk(s), not shy away from them

Leading from the front means you accept the risk(s), not shy away from them.

There are three dangers to leading from the front.

First, there is a real risk—physical, intellectual, or reputational—to the leader.

Second, the closer you are to the problem, the less perspective you have. It's harder to see the big picture from the front.

Third, if the leader is always leading from the front, there is no opportunity for the team to develop leadership experience.

As managers transform themselves into leaders, they continuously evaluate whether leading from the front is commensurate with the gain.

Continuously evaluate whether leading from the front is commensurate with the gain

Who's got the midwatch?

A submarine can shelter from a typhoon or a Nor'easter[21] by simply submerging deeper; if the water was deep enough, we could go under any storm.

Many years ago, my first submarine, *USS Nautilus (SSN 571)*, was on her way to Halifax, Nova Scotia, for a December port call. Two facts made this an exciting trip: first, to get to Halifax, due to the shoaling continental shelf, a submarine must transit on the surface for almost twelve hours. Second, the worst Nor'easter in a decade was upon us.

As the most recently qualified and least experienced Officer of the Deck, responsible for the safe direction of the ship while the Captain slept, I had the privilege of standing watch, just me and a lookout, in an exposed cockpit 25 feet off the water in waves

---

21 A Nor'easter is a large, intense cyclone in the western North Atlantic Ocean. Think about the final cataclysmic scene in the movie *The Perfect Storm* where the fishing boat is pitched end-over-end in the face of a 100-foot wave. Terrifying!

that easily topped 50 feet. Everyone else was warm and dry[22] in their bunks. More than 40 years later, I can still remember gleefully giving rudder and propulsion orders to surf the almost 4,000-ton *Nautilus* down the side of monster waves. In hindsight, great fun!

There was only one problem: Why was the youngest and least experienced person doing the most dangerous and hazardous task? The most senior watchstanders should have been up there, not the most junior.

When I was senior enough to make those kinds of choices, the toughest, most uncomfortable assignments always fell to the most senior.

> **The toughest, most uncomfortable assignments should always fall to the most senior**

You lead from the front.

Flying to DC in a Learjet, tin cup in hand

During the Great Recession, the Big 3 automakers were in trouble. No one was buying their cars, and they were hemorrhaging cash. What to do? Simple solution—ask for a government bailout. The CEOs trooped onto their luxury Learjets and flew from Detroit to DC to ask for a handout. Needless to say, this was not received well by lawmakers.[23] Those CEOs chose not to lead by example.

Poor leadership symbolism matters.

During the COVID pandemic, a remarkable number of CEOs cut their pay or chose not to take any compensation. They were asking their teams to take pay cuts, and in many cases, separation. These CEOs led from the front.

Great leadership symbolism matters.

---

22 Although the crew were warm and dry, most likely they were not particularly comfortable as *Nautilus* was pitching and rolling like crazy in the storm.

23 "There is a delicious irony in seeing private luxury jets flying into Washington, D.C., and people coming off of them with tin cups in their hand, saying that they're going to be trimming down and streamlining their businesses," Rep. Gary Ackerman (D-NY), told the chief executive officers of Ford, Chrysler, and General Motors at a hearing of the House Financial Services Committee.

Balance

There is a difference between a so-called leader who hogs the spotlight and one who leads from the front.

During the 2007 wildfires in San Diego County, Chair of the County Board of Supervisors Ron Roberts led twice-daily press conferences to update the 3 million-plus residents of San Diego County on the imminent fire threat to many of their homes and livelihoods. He was always generous with credit. He accepted that he did not know everything and never tried to answer a question he didn't know the answer to.

He balanced the symbolism of being in charge (in this case, of literally standing in front of the microphone and cameras) with the needs of his team and the needs of his stakeholders for accurate information.

Transforming managers into leaders

Like many transformations, this is a gradual change. As the manager evolves into a leader, they become more and more visible at the head of the group.

You lead from the front—physically, emotionally, reputationally, and intellectually!

KEYS TO THE TRANSFORMATION

As managers transform themselves into leaders, they:
- Are more and more visible—physically, emotionally, reputationally, and intellectually—at the *front* of the organization.
- Continuously evaluate whether leading from the front is commensurate with the gain.
- Continuously evaluate whether their leadership positioning is creating positive or negative symbolism.
- Proactively look for opportunities to lead by example.

WHAT AM I GOING TO DO DIFFERENTLY ON MONDAY TO TRANSFORM MYSELF FROM A MANAGER INTO A LEADER?

- Find one opportunity in the next month to lead from the front.

May the Force Be with You

Origin

The phrase originated in *Star Wars: Episode IV – A New Hope* and has continued as a part of the *Star Wars* genre ever since.

In *The Empire Strikes Back*, the young Jedi knight, Luke Skywalker, can't seem to accomplish a seemingly impossible task: lifting an X-wing fighter out of a swamp on Dagoba using only the mental energy of the Force. His teacher, Yoda, convinces Luke that having the Force on your side makes things like size and strength inconsequential. Once Luke *believes* he has the Force, he accomplishes the seemingly impossible—lifting the X-wing out of the swamp.

The concept

Leadership comes with responsibility, as discussed in chapter 7.

Leadership also comes with power and authority—the Force.

Like Luke in the movie, when leaders *think* they have the Force, they magically possess the Force and can accomplish amazing things.

Many managers, however, are reluctant to use that power and authority.

- ✓ Some are concerned that it makes them look authoritarian.
- ✓ Some don't know how to use their power and authority.
- ✓ Some are afraid of power and authority.
- ✓ Many don't know their power and authority.

On the other side of the coin, some managers abuse power and authority (they become petty tyrants).

Leaders walk a fine line—they use power and authority but don't abuse power and authority. But, of course, much easier said than done!

> **Leaders use, but not abuse, their power and authority**

Move the damn trash can

The following is an illustrative yet ridiculously mundane example. Four years after I started as the San Diego County Medical Society (SDCMS) CEO, we sold our old building and moved into a modern office suite. We replaced all our outdated furnishings and hardware. I moved into my brand-new office, reveling in that "new house" feel. The outfitters had randomly placed the trash can at the other end of my office from my desk. Why they did that, I have no clue.

When I wanted to toss something in the trash, I had to hit a trash can far from my desk. Now I'm not much of a basketball player, so I missed a lot. So, I would get up, go to the trash can, and slam dunk the trash from a couple of feet away. Score!

After a couple of weeks of abysmal shooting, with no improvement on the horizon, I asked myself, "Why the heck don't I move the trash can to within slam-dunk range of my desk?" So, of course, I did, and of course, my shooting percentage improved dramatically.

> **Managers have the power and authority, yet (often) don't use it**

This fable is not about trash cans—it's about power. I had the power, so why did I wait more than three minutes from my first failed shot to move the trash can? Decision inertia. I had the power, but I failed to use it. And so it goes with many more consequential decisions.

Managers have the power and authority, yet (often) don't use it. Leaders have the power and authority, and use it.

Start up the nuclear reactor!

Haddo, my second ship, was a victim of the Vietnam and post-Vietnam dual disasters of high operational tempo and few maintenance dollars. She was an engineering challenge.

One day, in a very tense operational environment, the nuclear reactor shut itself down. Not a good thing based on *Haddo*'s location. With the reactor not providing electrical power and no convenient shore power outlets to plug into, *Haddo* had to run a diesel generator as an alternate electrical power source. Unfortunately, the diesel is extremely loud and leaves a highly visible trail of smoke (extremely poor options given *Haddo*'s location).

There are well-established procedures and troubleshooting guides, but *Haddo*'s engineers couldn't find a cause for the shutdown. Everything checked out perfectly.

But the rules were clear: you don't start up the reactor until you know *why* it shut down.

Admiral Hyman Rickover, the inventor of the nuclear submarine, was a notorious stickler for procedural compliance. Don't follow the rules, and you get hammered or fired.

The Rickover rules were clear—keep troubleshooting.

But the Admiral also knew that sometimes you had to break (or change[24]) the rules. Paraphrasing Rickover, following the reactor plant procedures, and causing the submarine to sink, was dumb.

They kept on troubleshooting. Still couldn't find a thing wrong. Everything still checked out perfectly.

The manager (the Engineer Officer) said, "We need to keep troubleshooting until we find a cause. That's the rule!"

The leader (the Captain) ordered the Engineer to start up the reactor even though the cause had not yet been identified.

The Captain had been to an extensive course before assuming command that taught him both the rules, the reasons for the rules, and when and why he could (and should) break the rules. He was prepared to make the tough decision!

The Captain knew he could safely break one rule (that the cause for reactor shutdown must be *known* and corrected) to follow the more important rule (keep the ship and crew safe). Keeping the reactor shut down for further troubleshooting with no end in sight while running that noisy and smoky diesel in that operational environment was hazardous.

Exceptions

General David Petraeus, in his *12 Rules for Living*, said it beautifully: "There is an exception to every rule, standard operating procedure, and policy: it is up to the leaders to determine when exceptions should be made and to explain why they made them."

> **There is an exception to every rule, standard operating procedure, and policy**

---

24 Many believe that the loss of the submarine *USS Thresher* in 1963 was ultimately caused (preceded by a failure in the seawater systems and a malfunction in the air systems) by rigid adherence to a specific rule designed to protect the reactor, which placed the ship in lethal jeopardy by limiting propulsion during a flooding casualty. Rules were changed, and training emphasized the absolute need to maintain propulsion.

The leader has the power—they need to use it.

As managers transition to leaders, they know their power and authority better. They use that power and authority more and abuse it less.

May the force be with you! Use it for good.

KEYS TO THE TRANSFORMATION

As managers transition to leaders, they:
- Know their power(s) and authority.
- Know the underlying reasons for those power(s) and authority.
- Use their power(s) and authority more effectively.
- Thoughtfully break the rules when they have to.
- Abuse their power(s) and authority less.

WHAT AM I GOING TO DO DIFFERENTLY ON MONDAY TO TRANSFORM MYSELF FROM A MANAGER INTO A LEADER?

- Reflect on a past circumstance where you broke (or should have broken) a rule for the greater good.
- Write down at least three unwritten rules at home or at work.

3

SECTION 3

ACTIONING

Sooner or later, you have to do stuff. Leaders translate theory and talk into action.

Leaders approach action differently than managers.

This section presents five aphorisms that engender a bias to action, thereby transforming managers into leaders.

- *What are you going to do differently on Monday?* If you continuously ask yourself and others what will change as a result of your talking, writing, or thinking, then stuff gets done.
- *Plans are nothing. Planning is everything.* You have to focus on dynamic preparation. The verb, *planning*, is way more important than the noun, *plan*.

- *Improvise, adapt, and overcome.* You have to be flexible. Plans look great on paper, but reality is a harsh master. You and yours have to have the mental resilience to deal with the inevitable changes.
- *It is better to sweat in peace than bleed in war.* You and yours have to be trained well and trained realistically. Poor training is everywhere; it takes energy and intellect to design training that will prepare you and yours.
- *Why? Why? Why? Why? Why? Why?* You have to look for the root cause of problems and issues. Solving the proximate problem is seductively easy. Addressing the underlying root cause is much more challenging.

What Are You Going to Do Differently on Monday?

Origin

I'm not the first to come up with the phrase, but I'm going to take credit for it anyway!

The concept

I teach a one-year leadership and management seminar over 23 days, encompassing 54 sessions and 105 hours of instruction. We overwhelm students with knowledge, concepts, and ideas. But it's not enough to simply present lots of stuff; I want the scholars to do something with what they've seen and heard. So at the end of every session, I ask a simple question, "So, what are you going to do differently on Monday?"[25] Said a little differently, "How are you going to apply the knowledge that we've presented to your world?"

I've facilitated many strategic planning sessions. Almost without fail, we created marvelous and thoughtful documents, which often became shelfware.[26] Why? Because the participants

---

25 The course usually takes place on Thursday, Friday, and Saturday, so in this case, it's literally Monday. But Monday is really a metaphor for "soon."
26 Documents or plans that are put on the shelf to gather dust and result in no action.

never transitioned from plans to actions. As I became a more experienced leader of these sessions, I incorporated the plan's *implementation* into the process. And I repeatedly refocused the participants by asking the "Monday" question.

Asking "What are you going to do differently on Monday?" is a call to action.

Just one more study...
The head of the Air Force, General C.Q. Brown, said at his 2020 confirmation hearing:

> Anything we don't want to do, we study...That's a way of delaying a decision. There's a risk in taking a decision, and there's a risk in not taking a decision. In choosing not to choose, it defers a chance to move forward. At some point in any discussion, you're going to have to decide what to do.

We all will find seemingly excellent reasons, nay excuses, not to get something done! Fire the excuses[27] that keep you from acting.

Yeah, but I don't have all the facts
Managers thrive on certainty. They are conservative, and that, in and of itself, is not a bad thing. You want managers to make fact-based and data-driven decisions—sort of.

Regretfully, you will never have all the facts. You will never have all the data. You will never be 100 percent sure. And one more thing: you will never have all the time you need.

Leaders recognize that, in decision making, there is rarely certainty and they accept that they will likely never have all the facts, data, and time.

But leaders bound the uncertainty—they have a sense of the odds. And then, they evaluate their actions based on the odds and the risk. But they take action.

---

27 This concept is thoroughly explored in the book *Fire Your Excuses* by Drs. Bill Dyment and Marcus Dayhoff

For a submarine, there is (relative) safety in depth. Usually, but not always, while deep, submarines are immune to detection and immune to being run over by surface vessels. But, sooner or later, submarines have to come shallow enough to stick various extendable masts above the waves. Coming to periscope depth[28] *safely* is the signature skill of young submarine officers, akin to landing on an aircraft carrier *safely* for young naval aviators.

The ocean is messy. Information is not perfect. Sometimes you hear the supertanker, and sometimes you don't. Sometimes you hear the trawler, and sometimes you don't.

Deciding how much information to gather—and how long to collect that information—is a balancing act. You want enough data to be sure you don't hit (or get hit by) something. But you don't have all day (or all night). So in almost every case, you err on the side of caution.

And sometimes, it works out a little differently.

Off the coast of the Philippines on *Pogy*, we completely lost the navigational picture (the computer burped, as they sometimes do). Bad idea to not know our *exact* location when so close to land. So *Pogy* had to quickly reach periscope depth to regain the navigational picture. There were a million (or so it felt) fishing trawlers right on top of us. It was tense!

We accepted the risk (we *had* to get the navigation picture), we bounded the risk (we used sonar tools that we would typically not use), and we had the right people (I was the senior watchstander, and the Captain was right there). But we acted—we did not study the problem to death.

> **The transformation from manager to leader is about learning to accept uncertainty, bounding risk, and taking action**

---

28 So called because it is a depth where the tip of the periscope is above the waves.

The transformation from manager to leader is about learning to accept uncertainty, bounding risk, and taking action.

The manager-leader diad
One of the most effective diads in getting stuff done is to pair a great manager and a great leader.

At the Medical Society, I hired Jim Beaubeaux as my COO with the explicit understanding that he was the manager (he was brilliant at it), and I was the leader, and that we would try very hard to stay out of each other's way. We constantly pushed-pulled each other so that we always had two different perspectives on the same problem. The creative tension worked superbly.

> **The manager holds the leader back.
> The leader pulls the manager forward**

The manager holds the leader back by insisting that the leader not make fact-poor, data-poor, or impulsive decisions.

The leader pulls the manager forward by insisting on not taking forever and accepting a certain lack of data and facts.

Not everyone has the luxury of a brilliant manager like Jim at their elbow; sometimes, you and you alone have to both think like a manager *and* think like a leader.

The great American novelist F. Scott Fitzgerald said, "The test of a first-rate intelligence is the ability to hold two opposing ideas in mind at the same time and still retain the ability to function."

I would adapt Fitzgerald's aphorism to say the test of a first-rate leader is someone who can simultaneously think like a manager and act like a leader without going nuts. Admittedly, that statement is not as elegant as Fitzgerald's, but it points out the management-leadership duality.

> **A first-rate leader is someone who can simultaneously think like a manager and act like a leader**

It might be Monday, it might be next month, or it might be next year

The "Monday" in the maxim is symbolic and should not be taken literally.

In some cases, you should take action immediately. In other cases, action may take longer—sometimes significantly longer.

The real point is to incent forward motion vice stasis.

So, what are *you* going to do differently on Monday?

KEYS TO THE TRANSFORMATION

As managers transition to leaders, they:
- Learn to accept uncertainty, bound risk, and then take action.
- Avoid studying problems to death.
- Accept that you will only have some fraction of the information to make a decision.
- Think like a manager and act like a leader.

WHAT AM I GOING TO DO DIFFERENTLY ON MONDAY TO TRANSFORM MYSELF FROM A MANAGER INTO A LEADER?

- Ask, "What am I/you going to do differently today?"

Plans Are Nothing, Planning Is Everything

Origin

This aphorism is attributed to General (and later President) Dwight D. Eisenhower.

The concept

Plans is a noun. *Planning* is a verb. Eisenhower's message is quite simple: the act of planning is what matters. The final piece of paper (or file) reflects the act of planning, but it can (and will) change.

How is this different from the next chapter, "Improvise, Adapt, and Overcome"?

The two aphorisms are related but are not the same.

"Plans are nothing, planning is everything" focuses on preparation.

The next chapter, "Improvise, Adapt, and Overcome," focuses on what to do when (not if) the situation (and the plans) must change.

How does the planner transform into a leader?
Managers are usually proficient planners, but leaders must think well beyond what's on the piece of paper.

There are three aspects to "planning is everything" that are traits of leadership.

First, the leader questions the assumptions underlying the plan.

Second, the leader explores all the "What ifs?"

Finally, the leader insists on thinking through the actions if "What ifs?" come true. Said differently, what are the contingencies if things don't go per plan?

Managers transform themselves into leaders by actively planning, questioning the plan's underlying assumptions, aggressively probing the low probability–high impact possibilities, and developing contingencies.

Question the assumptions
All plans have assumptions. Some are explicit. Some are unspoken.

Managers will list the assumptions on a plan.

Leaders look beyond the explicit assumptions on the plan.

And leaders will question all the assumptions, written and unwritten.

Leaders question explicit and implicit assumptions

Japan has executed two surprise attacks in the last century, both occurring before a formal declaration of war. Pearl Harbor in 1941 is well known. Less well known is the surprise attack on the then Russian seaport of Port Arthur (present-day Dalian in China) to start the Russo-Japanese War in 1904.

Navy planners in the late 1930s assumed that the Pacific theater would be controlled by large battleship fleets sortieing from their secure homeports.

Geography matters. It turns out that Pearl Harbor, the supposedly secure homeport of the American Pacific fleet, is quite shallow and therefore (so it was assumed) not susceptible to air-dropped torpedoes.[29]

In November 1940, a small British carrier force flying antiquated biplanes, using specially modified air-dropped torpedoes designed to operate in shallow harbors, sank or damaged a number of Axis battleships in the well-protected and shallow harbor of Taranto, Italy.

While hindsight is always 20-20, consider that Navy senior leaders *did not ask*:

- ✓ If Japan executed one surprise attack to start a war, why would we *assume* they would not do it again?
- ✓ If the British could sink battleships in a shallow harbor, why would we *assume* that the Japanese would not use the exact same technical innovation?

> **Those who do not question assumptions—and learn from history—are doomed to repeat it**

This book is meant to help transform managers into leaders, not to recite naval history. Yet those who do not question assumptions—and learn from history—are doomed to repeat it (see chapter 22).

Well, "What if?"

A great technique to flush out the unspoken "What ifs?" is the Black Swan exercise.[30] It goes well beyond simply asking, "What could possible go wrong here?" Instead, it's asking, "What would happen if something that

> **"What would happen if something that has a low probability but high impact were to happen here?"**

---

29 Air-dropped torpedoes sink a significant distance before levelling out close to the surface.

30 Nassim Nicholas Taleb outlined the process and the reasoning for looking at the impact of the highly improbable in his bestseller, *The Black Swan*.

has a relatively low probability but a very high impact were to happen here?"

This is a transformational question because if that question were to be asked by anyone other than the leader, the questioner would be laughed off the podium.

I'm sure that the disaster manager who suggested that terrorists fly airplanes loaded with jet fuel into buildings was not taken seriously. How would history have turned out differently if the leader of disaster preparations had asked their team to explore that option and determine what could be done about it?

The nuance of the "What if?" questions, and what separates managers from leaders, is the weight given to the unlikely.

Scenario planning, first developed by Royal Dutch Shell,[31] popularized the process of examining all the possibilities and planning for them. Like all major oil companies, Royal Dutch Shell had to have a plan for building refineries and other capital-intensive infrastructure. If the price of oil is high, investing in costly refineries makes sense. Conversely, if the price of oil is low, then building more refineries doesn't pencil out. So far, pretty routine and well within the purview of a good manager.

Managers will ask mundane, albeit important, questions.

But it's the leader who has to ask really tough and innovative questions. In this case, things like:

- ✓ What would happen to the price of oil if we experienced a global health emergency that drove demand into the basement?
- ✓ What would happen to the price of oil if the Suez Canal or the Straits of Hormuz were blocked to tanker traffic by terrorists?
- ✓ What would happen if the Panama Canal had a mechanical failure that shut it down for six months?

---

31 The topic is addressed thoroughly in the book *Scenarios: The Art of Strategic Conversation*, by Kees van der Heijden

✓ What would happen to the price of oil if coastal nuclear power plants were severely damaged by a tsunami in the Pacific Ring of Fire[32] due to an earthquake of magnitude greater than 9.0?

And it's only the leader who can ask these low-probability, high-impact questions and not get either ignored or laughed off the podium.

Contingencies

Once the leader has questioned all the assumptions and listed all the high-risk/low-probability "What ifs?" then it is the manager who must create contingencies.

Regretfully, resources are not unlimited, so you cannot mitigate every possible bad outcome.

Leaders have to decide which contingencies to resource and why

Managers have to identify and cost out contingencies.

Leaders have to decide which contingencies to resource and why.

On my first deployment as Engineer Officer on *Pogy*, one of our big pumps failed in the middle of the Indian Ocean. Using some incredible ingenuity, we made a temporary repair[33] until we could get to a maintenance facility. I had a bad feeling about that critical pump; I knew it was an inanimate object, but I was sure it was out to get me! So prior to my next six-month deployment, I got creative. I finagled[34] a completely unauthorized spare pump and lashed it down in Engine Room Lower Level.

Fast-forward to our next deployment to the far reaches of the Pacific. When I walked my Captain's boss through the Engine Room, he was aghast. "What the h*** are you doing with that pump?" But, when I told him the story, he smiled and turned a

---
32 The rim of the Pacific has a very high probability of earthquakes, and is often referred to as the Rim of Fire due to its tectonic activity.
33 See chapter 12.
34 A highly technical phrase for extreme creativity.

blind eye.[35] And sure enough, in the middle of nowhere, the damn thing broke again. But this time, I had a spare. Problem solved!

Transforming yourself from a manager to a leader is all about prioritizing and resourcing your options. That's scary because if you decide to mitigate the wrong contingencies, that has a real-world negative impact.

Leaders have to be willing to ask hard questions and act on the answers!

> **Leaders ask hard questions and act on the answers**

The leader's focus is on the verb *planning*, not the noun *plans*.

---

[35] To *turn a blind eye* is often attributed to an incident in the life of Vice Admiral Horatio Nelson, who was blinded in one eye early in his Royal Navy career. During the Battle of Copenhagen in 1801 his timid boss sent a signal to Nelson's forces ordering them to discontinue the action. When this order was brought to the more aggressive Nelson's attention, he lifted his telescope to his blind eye, saying, "I have a right to be blind sometimes. I really do not see the signal," and most of his forces continued to press home the attack—successfully!

KEYS TO THE TRANSFORMATION

As managers transition to leaders, they:
- Focus on *planning*, not plans.
- Question a plan's underlying assumptions.
- Probe low-probability/high-impact possibilities.
- Develop contingencies.
- Prioritize and resource options.
- Think through the actions to be taken if one of the "What ifs?" becomes real.

WHAT AM I GOING TO DO DIFFERENTLY ON MONDAY TO TRANSFORM MYSELF FROM A MANAGER INTO A LEADER?

- Stress test the plan for one existing project to see whether the plan is robust enough to tolerate significant changes in circumstances.
- Examine the planning process for one future project to see whether low-probability but high-impact possibilities have been considered.

Improvise, Adapt, and Overcome

Origin

It wasn't a particularly great movie, unless, of course, you're a Clint Eastwood fan. *Heartbreak Ridge* follows a fictional grizzled Marine Gunnery Sergeant[36] and Medal of Honor winner, Tom Highway. He whips into shape a small, elite unit that had gone limp under previous leadership.

At the beginning of the movie, Gunny Highway growls at his team of slackers in that unique gravel-crusher voice: "You improvise. You adapt. You overcome."

The phrase has become one of the unofficial guiding principles of the Marine Corps.

---

36 Marine Corps Gunnery Sergeants and Navy Chief Petty Officers hold the rank of E-7 and form the backbone of the Marine Corps' and Navy's enlisted community. They are informally referred to as Gunny and Chief, respectively, a title many strive for and few achieve.

The concept

Things are not going to turn out the way you planned. | **Things are not going to turn out the way you planned**

Prussian Field Marshal Helmut von Moltke in the mid-19th century said it perfectly as it applies to warfare: "No plan ever survives first contact with the enemy."

Many have adapted that saying to non-military situations to read, "No plan ever survives first contact with reality."

~~Japan~~ Korea

Submarines are incredibly complex tools operating in two hostile environments, the ocean and the enemy. Even when they deploy to the far reaches of the world, they still require regular maintenance. The crew performs a lot of the minor maintenance, and quite a bit can be done underway. But, every three or four months, you just have to tie up to the pier for a couple of weeks and do major maintenance.

These maintenance periods require extensive planning (writing work packages, ordering parts, detailed scheduling to minimize conflicts, etc...). You don't just drive up to the dealership and throw them the keys!

The submarine I was Engineer Officer of, *Pogy,* was scheduled for mid-deployment upkeep in Japan. We were ready; everything was teed up as a result of a month of detailed planning and preparation. Thirty-six hours before arriving in Japan, the plan changed. We were going to Korea instead of Japan. Completely different maintenance facility. Completely different capabilities. Completely different darn near everything. Everything had to be rethought, rewritten, and rescheduled—in 36 hours. We had to adapt and overcome.

Cathy, my wife, had plane tickets and visas to visit me in Japan (and had even practiced her rudimentary Japanese phrases). She got the call about the same time I did and pivoted from Japan to Korea in under two days. New flights, new travel arrangements, new language books.[37] She had to improvise.

Things will change. You have two choices—complain/whine/dither or improvise/adapt/overcome.

Pogy got her maintenance, and Cathy and I had a fabulous five days exploring Korea during my leave.

Change the attitude

The transformation from manager to leader involves three fundamental attitudinal shifts.

First, the questioning attitude that proactively examines what could possibly go wrong here.

Second, the mental resilience to accept, with a positive attitude, that your well-laid-out plan is going to change.

Third, the creativity to come up with novel solutions to new problems.

The questioning attitude—prepare for things to go wrong

Here's one of my favorite questions: "What could possibly go wrong here?"

There are many techniques and processes that great leaders have at their disposal to think about what could go wrong and how to prevent things from going wrong.

Leaders encourage, nay demand, those techniques and processes.

If you ask your team to lay out possible failure points and stimulate their thinking about preparing for those options, they will be (mostly) ready for things to go wrong.

> **What could possibly go wrong here?**

The transformational change from manager to leader is that constantly questioning attitude about what could go wrong.

---

37 Luckily no need for a new visa, as Korea didn't require them.

Mental resilience—Semper Gumby

The Marine Corps motto since 1883 has been *Semper Fidelis,* Latin for "always faithful."

Gumby is a Claymation™ creation that is very flexible and has a special knack for getting into, out of, and through fantastic and often danger-filled escapades.

Semper Gumby, a concatenation of the two ideas and phrases, became a watchword for many in the service who had to continuously adapt to rapidly changing and often hazardous conditions.

But *Semper Gumby* is so much more than a phrase—it's an attitude.

The transformational change from manager to leader is to embrace *Semper Gumby.* Leaders model the mental resilience, the good humor, and the positivity that encourages the team rather than depresses them when, not if, things go wrong.

Get me all the pencils

On *Pogy*, in the middle of the Indian Ocean (a really, really long way from anywhere), I received the unpleasant news that a very large pump, one of only two that moved water around the ship, sounded like a dying washing machine and needed a new bearing.[38] Shortly thereafter, it died. Dead. Frozen. It wouldn't turn with a crowbar.

We needed a new bearing.

Okay, pull out a new bearing from supply... we have those, right? No problem. Oh wait... big problem. The replacement bearing was rusted through because, for whatever reason (we never did find out why), the part we had in stock was bad, and the nearest parts warehouse was about 3,000 miles away. In another ocean.

Now what?

---

38 A bearing keeps a rotating shaft in place and minimizes friction.

When given license and incentive to improvise, one of my insanely creative mechanics came up with the brilliant idea of making our own bearing. Out of graphite.[39] We could improvise a mold, melt the graphite, pour it into the mold, and presto—temporary bearing. Not perfect, not a long-term fix, but it would get us to the next pit stop and a visit to the express line at the submarine parts warehouse.

Okay, where's the graphite? Ummm, we don't... Oh wait, we have a bajillion pencils, and pencil lead is graphite! For the next couple of days, the entire crew was scavenging pencils, shaving off the wood, melting the lead, and the next thing you know, the pump was running again.

The transformational change from manager to leader is to encourage creativity and improvisation from your team.

Improvise, adapt, and overcome.

---

39 Graphite is a common bearing material that allows a rotating element, the shaft, to rub with little or no friction against a stationary element, the bearing, thereby keeping the shaft steady.

KEYS TO THE TRANSFORMATION

As managers transition to leaders, they:
- Develop a questioning attitude that proactively examines what could possibly go wrong.
- Adopt the mental resilience to accept with a positive attitude that your well-laid-out plan is going to change.
- Embrace the maxim "Improvise, Adapt, Overcome" by encouraging creativity and innovation to arrive at novel solutions to new problems.

WHAT AM I GOING TO DO DIFFERENTLY ON MONDAY TO TRANSFORM MYSELF FROM A MANAGER INTO A LEADER?

- For a project in process, re-look at what could go wrong.
- When, not if, a well-laid plan needs radical re-arrangement, encourage your team to "Improvise, Adapt, and Overcome."

It Is Better to Sweat in Peace than Bleed in War

Origin

Most recently, this aphorism is attributed to General Norman Schwarzkopf, commander of coalition forces during Kuwait's liberation during Desert Storm 1. However, many have been similarly quoted, as far back as the Spartans in ancient Greece.[40]

The concept

This quote applies to so much more than military conflict. Any individual or organization that deals with stressful situations must take this guidance to heart. This guidance is essentially applicable to anyone and everyone.

The central idea of this maxim is effective preparation.

Managers who successfully transform themselves into leaders apply this aphorism in at least two ways:

- ✓ Preparation for conflict or stress, whether armed or unarmed, is not treated as an option.
- ✓ The more realistic the preparation, the higher the probability of success.

---

40 "He who sweats more in training bleeds less in war."—Spartan Warrior Creed

Preparation

Many trainings or preparations are mandated by a well-intentioned subset of the organization: the training department. As a staff function, they assess the needs and create the necessary training to cope with those needs.

Many managers have assigned training to the in-house department or outsourced it to consultants or training providers.

As managers transform themselves into leaders, they insource training. However, many leaders take preparation so seriously that they make training the current (and following) generation a personal priority.

As CEO of the Medical Society, I quickly discovered that physicians had little or no leadership and management training. Doctors are among the most intelligent people in any room, but the medical training pipeline allotted zero time to prepare them for leadership or management roles.

To correct this gap, we developed a two-day course that provided interested physicians with the basic background, references, and critical concepts necessary to become leaders and/or managers.[41]

Checking the box

When managers delegate training to the training department, the results are usually mixed. Some training is better than none, but training run by an outsider usually just checks the box.

Often the training is passive, not active. For example, watching an internet video while multitasking is not effective training. Taking a simplistic multiple-guess test demonstrates very little. Likewise, reading a simplified text is likely a wasted effort.

The Missouri state motto has it right: "Show me." Effective training is experiential. Effective training is active. Training effectiveness is evaluated by demonstrating a skill or knowledge

---

[41] That course, and the demonstrable need for the material, became the inspiration for this and my previous two books.

> **A leader makes sure that the skill is demonstrated under as close-to-real circumstances as possible** under the identical stressors as the trainees will see in real life.
>
> A manager makes sure the box is checked.

A leader makes sure that the skill is demonstrated under as close-to-real circumstances as possible.

Realism

The most effective training is realistic. An oft-repeated and time-tested conflict-based maxim is "Train like you fight, fight like you train."

The more a manager transforms into a leader, the more realistic the training they provide.

Great leaders will go to incredible lengths to ensure that the training environment is almost identical to the real environment. Ideally, the training environment should be more challenging than the real thing.

Here's an example from my time at the Medical Society. Legislators and their staffs are usually well-intentioned, but healthcare legislation is often written with inadequate input from those who will be most affected by it—doctors and patients. The people writing the bills need to hear the voices of doctors and patients (this is also known as lobbying).

Yet lobbying is not a skill taught at medical school. So we had to create a training regime that would prepare doctors, omnipotent in the exam room, to speak to elected representatives, omnipotent in their Capitol offices.

> **Train like you fight and fight like you train** One option was to have our trainee lobbyists read articles on effective lobbying and speak to retired Capitol veterans. Lame!

Instead, we set up video cameras and had our trainee lobbyists speak to "mock" elected officials—usually highly experienced doctors or staff who had seen every trick in the book. And the mock-electeds were neither friendly nor kind. We made it hard and harder, then we reviewed the video and did it again. It was grueling, humbling, and highly effective. When the doctors pitched the electeds for real, it was almost always much easier than the drill.

You sweat in peace so you don't bleed in war. You train like you fight and fight like you train.

As managers transition themselves to leaders, the training becomes more realistic and more effective.

KEYS TO THE TRANSFORMATION

As managers transition to leaders, they:
- Actively pursue insourcing training to their organization (and not the training department).
- Make the preparation as realistic as possible.
- Measure the effectiveness of training against real-world standards.

WHAT AM I GOING TO DO DIFFERENTLY ON MONDAY TO TRANSFORM MYSELF FROM A MANAGER INTO A LEADER?

- Initiate a complete review of your training program, including the training subjects, the training method, and the measurement of training effectiveness.
- Make it a point to attend several training sessions each month.

Why? Why? Why? Why? Why? Why?

Origin

The inventor of the nuclear-powered submarine, Admiral Hyman Rickover, was implacable in his search for truth and would ask, "Why?" until he reached the bedrock of causality.[42]

The concept

Problems happen. Things break. Stuff doesn't work. People misbehave. Groups fail.

As discussed in a previous chapter, nothing works out exactly per plan—it's the natural order of things.

Managers and leaders get paid to fix and prevent problems.

Regretfully, you can't fix what's broken or prevent what might break until you know what *really* happened and why.

This wisdom emphasizes that remediation is impossible until you know what happened, why the gizmo really broke, or why the group failed.

> **Remediation is impossible until you know what really happened**

---

[42] He is rumored to have said that the first five "whys" belonged to him, but the sixth "why" belongs to God.

Digging to bedrock

A manager will dig—but often not far enough. A leader digs until they find out the fundamental cause.

Here's an example from my experience as the president of a homeowner's association (HOA) board. The board receives the financials every month, including a listing of every check sent out for that month and that fiscal year. The checks are grouped by major categories, for example, "Building Repair."

One month I noted a large check for plumbing repairs.

- ✓ "Why" #1: I called the property manager, a very thoughtful and effective manager, and asked why the large bill? Answer: this was the cost of cleaning out a badly clogged sanitary drain for a specific unit. Okay, that seemed like a pretty good explanation, albeit a tad expensive. But it tickled my instincts.
- ✓ "Why" #2: How many other units required this rather costly solution to a plugged drain? I could look that up myself in the financials—and discovered that there had been several in the past months. Hmmmmm. Something is not right here.

Shortly after that, a vertical sewage line from an upper floor to a lower floor plugged up and overflowed yucky stuff into a unit. Something was *fundamentally* not right here.

- ✓ "Why" #3: I asked the property manager to find out the last time that the sewage lines for the *entire* building had been cleaned out. Answer: never, in the 20-year history of the building. Yikes!

I only had to go to three whys to get to causality. However, our property manager never alerted on the trend and the root cause. He was focused on fixing what was currently broken, not the root cause of the problem.

Managers fix symptoms. Leaders identify and fix the underlying causes of problems.

Misdirection

Closely related to not digging deep enough is misdirection. Not infrequently, the cause assigned to an event is wrong—sometimes inadvertently, sometimes deliberately.

Managers are less willing to challenge an erroneous cause.

Leaders develop a sixth sense when something just doesn't feel right and are single-minded in following up on their intuition.

> **Leaders develop a sixth sense when something just doesn't feel right**

Many times I've heard my inner voice say, *This just doesn't seem right*—and have ignored that voice at my peril.

Here's another mundane yet illustrative problem from my HOA experience. One of our three Jacuzzi spas wasn't working right. Rather than provide soothing jets of water, fantastic after a tough day, this one just blew air bubbles. For months, I discussed this with the management team, who felt the problem was associated with the system's design and was not fixable.

That just didn't feel right. While there are always exceptions, in general, people do not design systems to fail. Something, or someone, usually mucks systems up so that they don't behave as designed.

> **People do not design systems to fail**

Keep looking, I directed. The proposed answer was facile and not logical. Jacuzzis are meant to produce jets of water, not streams of air bubbles.

And sure enough, after I resisted the misdirection for months, we found the problem: someone in the far past had monkeyed with the pipes and created a hydraulic condition that prevented the proper operation.

Once we knew the root cause of the problem, the solution was easy.

> **Leaders resist the easy answer and the superficial explanation. They dig until they find the bedrock of causality**

Leaders resist the easy answer and the superficial explanation. They dig until they find the bedrock of causality.

We have met the enemy, and it is us

Pogo, Walt Kelly's long-running cartoon strip, famously declared, "We have met the enemy, and he is us."[43]

Managers, certainly bad ones, are often unwilling to accept that the actual cause for something gone wrong may very well have been themselves.

Leaders look hard at how *they* have contributed to a particular issue and are the first to accept that *they* may be the fundamental problem.

Let's say that you are in charge of an accounting department and that your team made an egregious error resulting in a significant and incorrect overpayment.

Let's review what happened. You asked the most junior of your Accounts Payable (AP) team, Caroline, to come in over the weekend to handle a very complex account. The multi-million-dollar account, normally

> **Leaders look hard at how *they* have contributed to a particular issue and are the first to accept that *they* may be the fundamental problem**

managed by your most senior AP person, Julie, was not only significantly in arrears but also the subject of litigation. But, Julie had to leave town because of a death in the family. Caroline, a hardworking and enthusiastic recruit from a prestigious honors accounting program, was the only person who volunteered to come in.

Regretfully, she made a mistake—a big one.

Now, who's to blame? Well, obviously, the junior person made a mistake. Blaming the innocent juniors is a (sadly) time-tested practice (just watch some of the back episodes of *The Office* or read the most recent *Dilbert* strip).

---

43 The cartoon shows a distraught Pogo staring at an ecological mess in 1971.

- ✓ A poor manager would shift the blame totally to Caroline.
- ✓ A good manager would realize they had something to do with the problem. Julie, the regular account manager, shares some blame as she left things in a state where a crisis was inevitable.
- ✓ A leader would accept full blame (and responsibility) since they set Caroline up to fail and let Julie's work on a critical account slip.

The leader failed Caroline on several fronts:

- ✓ The leader allowed a significant account to go into arrears.
- ✓ The leader did not have systems and processes to alert to a major AP problem.
- ✓ The leader did not brief Caroline adequately before sending her in on the weekend, with no one to ask for help.
- ✓ The leader did not set a tripwire (for example, telling Caroline to call the leader with her calculations before issuing the check).
- ✓ The leader did not go in personally on the weekend. This was not a routine transaction, and the boss needed to attend to the non-routine stuff.

A leader first asks themself, "How did I contribute to this problem, by either action or inaction?"

A leader keeps asking "why" until they expose all the problems, not just the ones close to the surface.

KEYS TO THE TRANSFORMATION

As managers transition to leaders, they:
- Develop a mindset of curiosity.
- Focus more and more on the underlying cause(s) rather than the symptoms.
- Resist the urge to accept facile answers that ignore common sense.
- Cultivate a sixth sense when something just doesn't feel right.
- Resist the urge to simply blame the obvious miscreant.

WHAT AM I GOING TO DO DIFFERENTLY ON MONDAY TO TRANSFORM MYSELF FROM A MANAGER INTO A LEADER?

- Probe deeper into a current problem or crisis to look for the bedrock of causality.
- After the next crisis, ask yourself, "How did I contribute to this problem, by either action or inaction?"

SECTION 4

PHILOSOPHIZING

The previous section was on actioning: the *what*.

This section is on philosophy and culture: the *how*.

Managers are rightly focused on action—getting stuff done.

As managers transition to leaders, they develop a clear, articulable philosophical core that tells the leader and followers *how* to get stuff done.

Not surprisingly, this section is the longest of the six. Philosophy/culture trumps nearly everything else in leadership and management. These seven wisdoms are certainly not the only ideas that will transition you from management to leadership, but they are *my* top seven.

- *Do what you can, with what you have, where you are at.* Theodore Roosevelt's oft-repeated dictum is a combination of a *call to action* and a *call to acceptance* of the world as it is. Managers complain about sub-optimal circumstances. Leaders work around and through them.
- *Nothing hard is ever easy.* Leaders become more inclined to tell the truth to themselves and their teams; accepting that hard stuff will be hard, no matter how smart or hardworking you are, is the first step.
- *What's the right thing to do here?* Absent a strong moral compass, leaders are (eventually) doomed. As managers transition to leadership, they self-reflect about what is right instead of what is convenient.
- *Life is tough, but it's tougher if you're not smart.* Regretfully, stupidity is ever-present. Managers rail about stupidity. Leaders are proactive in preventing and mitigating stupidity.
- *KISS—Keep It Simple & Short.* As managers transition to leaders, they start to cultivate the power of simplicity.
- *Perpetual optimism is a force multiplier.* The transition from management to leadership is driven by positivity.
- *Everything is connected to everything else.* As managers transition to leadership, they look for and use the interrelationships between the pieces, seeing the whole in addition to the parts.

Do What You Can, with What You've Got, Where You Are At

Origin

This quote comes from *Theodore Roosevelt: An Autobiography*, where Teddy quoted Bill Widener of Widener's Valley, Virginia.

The concept

Roosevelt's quote is about both activism and acceptance.

"Do what you can..." is a call to action.

You cannot change the entire world, but you can change that part of the world you influence. Stephen Covey in *The 7 Habits of Highly Effective People* speaks to a circle of influence (a space where you *can* make changes and take action) and a circle of concern (a space where you would *like to* make changes or take action). For most managers and leaders, their circle of influence is usually smaller than their circle of concern. However, leaders do two things better than managers:
- ✓ In the short-term, they accept, *with good grace*, their circle of influence and take action within it.
- ✓ In the medium- and long-term, they proactively seek to expand their circle of influence to match their circle of concern.

"...With what you've got, where you are at" is a call to acceptance. Yes, things would be better with greater resources. Yes, things would be better if you lived in Beverly Hills (or perhaps not...). But you cannot, in the immediate short-term, change many things. Long-term, yes. Short-term, no.

My interpretation of Roosevelt's wisdom is that you accept gracefully and act forcefully.

Serenity

The Serenity Prayer, credited to American theologian Reinhold Niebuhr, parallels Roosevelt's philosophy:

> May God grant me the serenity to accept the things I cannot change, the courage to change the things I can, and the wisdom to know the difference.

As managers become leaders, Niebuhr's voice speaks to them in three ways:
- ✓ Leaders must have the wisdom to know what they cannot (immediately) change.
- ✓ Leaders must have the courage to act on the things they can.
- ✓ And leaders must accept what is not (in the short-term) changeable.

But my boss doesn't get it...

I direct and teach parts of a one-year course on leadership and management for up-and-coming middle-level professionals at a large academic medical center.

Most participants are aspiring leaders but are still constrained by their managerial or clinical roles. They are over-the-top enthusiastic about putting their newfound knowledge and skills to work.

After a class segment, they often come back lamenting that they cannot get anything done because of the active or passive intransigence of their boss (or bosses).

Frequently, I share Roosevelt's quote and suggest to them the following:

- ✓ You are not likely to change a senior or manager in the organization with your brilliant new ideas. Most are set in their ways.
- ✓ Trying to move an immovable object will give you a headache or a hernia, so don't try more than a couple of times. But do try.
- ✓ Focus on what you can change—the people who work for and with you.
- ✓ Focus on change within the procedural and process constraints that you can change.
- ✓ Let your results speak for themselves.

You can't change the weather, you can only dress for it!
I debated whether to make this a separate truth but finally decided that this maxim overlaps and amplifies Roosevelt's wisdom.

In my younger days, I did a lot of hiking and backpacking in places where the weather wasn't always cooperative. No matter how hard I wanted it to stop raining or snowing, all I could do was to put on my rain gear, dress warmly, and wait for it to stop.

And so it is with many things as a leader.

As you transform from manager to leader, you will become more accepting that you cannot change many conditions in your world—just like you can't stop the rain.

As you transform yourself from manager to leader, you focus on preparing for inclement conditions: buy a figurative umbrella, dress in your figurative raincoat, pore over the figurative weather report before it pours, etc.

And finally, the more of a leader you become, the more you will focus on *accurate* weather reports[44] (hint: none are perfect, but many will give you a sense of what's coming!).

But above all, do what you can, where you are at, with what you have.

---

44 Speaking metaphorically, of course.

KEYS TO THE TRANSFORMATION

As managers transition to leaders, they:
- Become more accepting that they cannot change the entire world.
- Focus on changing that part of the world they influence.
- Expand their influence.

WHAT AM I GOING TO DO DIFFERENTLY ON MONDAY TO TRANSFORM MYSELF FROM A MANAGER INTO A LEADER?

- Actively adopt a mindset of accepting gracefully and acting forcefully.
- Actively adopt a mindset that you can't change the weather, but you can dress for it. And you should listen to the weather report.

Nothing Hard Is Ever Easy

Origin

I'm sure this aphorism has been widely circulated, but I first heard it from my Executive Officer on *Haddo,* then-Commander Corky Corcoran.

The concept

A leader will face adversity. Many days, and nights, will be tough.

Fooling yourself into thinking that something you know will be hard is somehow magically going to be easy is being dishonest with yourself.

Worse, fooling your team by claiming that something you know will be hard is magically going to be easy is being dishonest.

Leaders must be honest with themselves and with their team.

Rode hard and put away wet

I reported to my second submarine in March of 1980 as the Weapons Officer.[45] For nearly a decade, *Haddo* had been rode hard and put away wet.[46]

The results were predictable. Very little worked right, no one gave a damn, and adversity was around every corner. The enlisted were all ready to go home. Alcoholism was everywhere. The Engineer was fired. The Navigator was incompetent. It was brutal.

My first ship, *Nautilus,* was a much bigger maintenance headache than *Haddo*. Still, she had an elite crew—no officer came to *Nautilus* unless Admiral Rickover and his team had handpicked them. *Haddo*, not so much.

I was smart, hardworking, knowledgeable, and incredibly frustrated. No matter how hard I worked or how late I stayed, it did not feel like I was making progress. I expected things to be easy because I was smart, hardworking, and knowledgeable.

Corky Corcoran, my very wise XO, sat me down one day (as I was ready to quit) and gave me the advice I've carried in my head ever since.

Nothing hard is ever easy.

The first time I heard that I nearly laughed in his face. Then I thought about it some more. Acceptance that *Haddo* was going to be hard, really hard, that progress was going to be slow, that we would have to shovel a lot of poop, helped me cope.

Haddo was not my desired normal, but it was *my* normal. And I was not the problem—the ship and the times were the problems.

---

[45] There are five senior officers on a submarine: Captain, Executive Officer, Engineer, Navigator, and Weapons Officer.
[46] The inadvisable practice of riding a horse to the point of exhaustion, and then stabling it while it is still coated in sweat, rather than allowing it to stand outside and dry off.

Humor as a salve

Since most of the officers on *Haddo* were young and cynical, we quickly coined a riff on "nothing hard is ever easy": "around here (*Haddo*), nothing easy is ever easy." Humor is just another way to cope. Leaders encourage it!

Tell the truth, always

My first Commanding Officer on *Pogy*, Commander (later four-star Admiral) Archie Clemins, often riffed on a quote attributed to Abraham Lincoln:

> You can fool all the people some of the time, and some of the people all the time, but you cannot fool all the people all the time.

He often told his officers, and acted accordingly, that you really can't fool any of the people any of the time. He was spot-on.

"Nothing hard is ever easy" is about telling the truth to yourself and your team.

Nothing hard is ever easy. Be realistic, but not pessimistic!

KEYS TO THE TRANSFORMATION

As managers transition to leaders, they:
- Accept that difficulties are difficult.
- Appreciate that all the talent in the world is not going to magically change hard to easy.
- Keep their sense of humor.

WHAT AM I GOING TO DO DIFFERENTLY ON MONDAY TO TRANSFORM MYSELF FROM A MANAGER INTO A LEADER?

- Change your perspective on one tough problem away from *moaning* about how hard it is to *accepting* that it's tough.
- Share your perspective with your team, and encourage them to be realistic but not pessimistic.

What's the Right Thing to Do Here?

Origin

General Norman Schwarzkopf said: "You always know the right thing to do. The hard part is doing it."

The actor Ben Kingsley, in a movie called *The Confession,* said: "What's hard is knowing what the right thing to do is. Once you know that, and believe it, doing the right thing is easy."

I combined the two thoughts into a simple question that leaders must ask themselves every hour of every day: "What's the right thing to do here?"

The concept

The Kingsley and Schwarzkopf quotations above seem to point in entirely different directions. So, which is it—do we always know the right thing, i.e., is knowing the right thing easy—or is knowing the right thing hard?

Yes. Both. Welcome to leadership.

23 TRUTHS THAT TRANSFORM MANAGERS INTO LEADERS

Unless they grew up in a toxic corporate environment (think Enron) or were raised by sociopaths, managers and leaders have been inculcated with values and ethics.[47] Because of cultural differences, not everyone has precisely the same ethics and values, but the basics are likely there. Most of us instinctively know the difference between right and wrong.

Schwarzkopf's concept is that we instinctively know where to go when presented with a choice between right and wrong, even if that choice has difficult ramifications.

> **Leaders instinctively know where to go when presented with a choice between right and wrong, even if that choice has difficult ramifications**

Kingsley's concept is that it's difficult to choose between two right things or two wrong things, sometimes horrendously so.

Knowing the right thing to do

Transforming yourself to a leader is all about knowing and *living* your values and ethics, *particularly* when it's hard.

I was raised with two ethical pillars: the Golden Rule (Do unto others as you would have done to you), and you will not lie, cheat, or steal.

As CEO, to amplify my expectations and to be specific, I wrote a two-page document for my team and myself, which I referred to as the CEO's Philosophy.[48]

We had a small team at the time. Not everyone was excelling. My COO and I were gradually correcting team members' suboptimal behaviors using the CEO's philosophy document. Everyone appeared to be "getting it," and I was not about to terminate any of them any time soon.

---

47 Regretfully, there is a long list of leaders who have neither ethics nor values. If you are working for or with a sociopath, and you are able, no matter the inducements to stay, get the hell out of their clutches.
48 My version, unchanged from 2015 when I retired, is attached as appendix 4. Please feel free to plagiarize it as you wish.

One of my team was caught in a lie. There was not a shred of doubt that she had lied—it was blatant.

My choice was clear, even though hard on myself and the team. I had invested a lot of time working with her to improve her performance. We would have a difficult time quickly replacing her, other team members would have to cover her position (more work...), and it would cost us both money and time to hire her replacement.

I fired her that afternoon.

Knowing the right thing to do was easy; doing the right thing was hard.

When your ethics conflict with the rules

Almost all organizations have written rules. Managers know that rule book inside and out.

Most organizations also have unwritten rules. Great managers know that rule book too.

Sometimes (more frequently than you'd think), your ethics and values will conflict with a written or unwritten rule.

Transforming yourself from a manager to a leader is all about knowing and living your values and ethics, *particularly* when those values and ethics conflict with the rules, written and unwritten.

> **Leaders live their values and ethics, *particularly* when those values and ethics conflict with the rules, written and unwritten**

Your choices when your ethics and values conflict with the rules are straightforward:

- ✓ Follow the rules, and violate your values and ethics, or
- ✓ Break the rule(s), and suffer the consequences, or
- ✓ Resign/quit, or
- ✓ Change the rule(s)

While the choices are not as excruciating as Sophie's Choice (discussed later in this chapter), this is nonetheless a tough set of options.

As you transform yourself from manager to leader, you will see more and more of these conflicts between the rules and your ethics.

While each is different, and history is replete with these tough choices, the only wrong answer is to favor the rules over your ethics and values.

What if the choice is less clear?
Kingsley's quote reminds me that there are two possibilities when the choice is *not* between right and wrong:

- ✓ Choosing between two bad things, the proverbial lesser of two evils.
- ✓ Choosing between two good things.

Choosing between two awful choices
In the movie *Sophie's Choice*, a young Polish mother in the claws of Hitler's Final Solution is forced to choose which of her two children will go to the gas chambers and which one will live. The choice is so awful that it has become synonymous with horrible options.

As you transform yourself from manager to leader, be prepared to make choices where there are no winners.

> **Be prepared to make choices where there are no winners**

Many CEOs and leaders during the COVID crisis had to make Sophie's Choices.

- ✓ Do I let 30 percent of my workforce go, knowing they will likely go hungry or worse?
- ✓ Do I cut everyone's paycheck by 30 percent, knowing that many will not be able to pay the rent?

My advice is simplistic, deliberately so. Consult your trusted few and your significant other, meditate on your decision in the context of your values, and then quickly[49] announce your decision and your reasoning.

Choosing between two good things
This is a great place to be, and I wish you many, many of those choices.

If it feels wrong, it probably is
If something seems wrong, and you have a gnawing feeling that something's not right, listen carefully to your inner voice.

If it feels wrong, it probably is.

Learning to listen to and trust your inner voice(s) is part of transforming yourself from a manager to a leader.

> **Listen very carefully to your inner voice**

After serving as CEO of the Medical Society for more than a decade, I kept hearing myself say that it was time to retire. "My work here is done," is what the little voice kept saying to me.

One of my biggest professional mistakes was not listening to that little voice earlier and taking too long to leave.

Is this moral, legal, and ethical?
As you transform from manager to leader, you will face more and more difficult choices. A great question to ask yourself is, "Is this moral, legal, and ethical?"

Ask this question of your team. Of course, you probably already know the answer, but speaking the question and hearing the answer will reinforce your thinking and help you make better decisions. And involving your team in these tough decisions teaches them your thinking and validates the decision.

---

49 Bad news never gets better with age.

You gotta pick a life jacket

There is an apocryphal story about a Navy leader who could not make a decision. His subordinates would joke that if this non-decider ever had to jump overboard, and someone threw him two life jackets, he would drown because he could not make up his mind.

Pick a life jacket. Make the darn decision. Do the right thing, even if it's hard.

KEYS TO THE TRANSFORMATION

As managers transition to leaders, they:
- Know, live, and articulate their values and ethics in the face of more and more difficult decisions.
- Are prepared to make choices where there are no winners.
- Are ready to make choices that trump the written and unwritten rules.
- Learn to tune in and trust their inner voices.

WHAT AM I GOING TO DO DIFFERENTLY ON MONDAY TO TRANSFORM MYSELF FROM A MANAGER INTO A LEADER?

- At the next major difficult decision, ask out loud, "Is this the right thing to do?"
- At the next major difficult decision, ask out loud, "Is this (decision) moral, legal, and ethical?"

Life Is Tough, but It's Tougher If You're Not Smart

Origin

This sanitized[50] paraphrase is misattributed to the actor John Wayne as Marine Sergeant John Stryker in the movie *The Sands of Iwo Jima*. Well, it does sound like something John Wayne would say!

The unsanitized quote is correctly attributed to the mid-70s movie *The Friends of Eddie Coyle*.

The concept

Mistakes happen.

Very few people get up in the morning and say to themselves, "Today, I'm going to do a bad job."

Most people get up every morning and want to do a great job.

And when they cannot do great work because of flawed processes or inadequate systems, that's not their fault. Most

> Most mistakes are not caused by stupidity but by poor design or implementation

---

50 It's rare to footnote a title, but the less tactful version of the quote is "Life is tough, but it's tougher if you're stupid." I went with more tactful!

mistakes are not caused by stupidity but by poor design or implementation.

There are, regretfully, some small fraction of people in any particular ecosystem who are dumb. Not malicious, just not smart. There is a bell curve of human intelligence, and some people are on the wrong side of the curve.

In addition, in any particular ecosystem, there is some fraction of people who are malicious. Human beings run the gamut, and some are just not good people.

I arbitrarily[51] call this the rule of 95/3/2, dividing people into three groups:

- ✓ 95 percent want to do a great job, and if they can't, it's usually inadequate systems or processes.
- ✓ 3 percent are misdemeanor stupid. Even with good processes and systems, they don't have the mental acuity to get the job done correctly.
- ✓ 2 percent are felony sociopaths. They will deliberately muck things up.

For the 95 percent...
If things go wrong, assume it's the process, not the people. Even if it looks like the people, dig very deep (see chapter 14) to make absolutely sure it's not the process.

As managers transform themselves into leaders, they dig deeper into mistakes and are less likely to simply blame *just* the people.

Several years ago, two Navy destroyers had separate collisions with freighters within months of each other in the Western Pacific. Sailors killed, ships crumpled, and careers ruined.

The initial response was to blame the watchstanders and the respective captains. The watchstanders did not follow standing orders and deserved the blame, and the Captain is always responsible for everything on their ship (see chapter 7).

---

[51] The percentages above are totally arbitrary, but they reflect that most people want to do well, some can't, and a few won't.

The Navy is unforgiving about collisions and groundings. Thou shalt not. Period.

But top Navy leaders started asking harder questions. Why exactly did intelligent people make stupid mistakes on two separate ships within months?

The answer turned out to be simple: the ships and crews were being asked to do too much and not given enough time to train. That simple fact caused top Navy leaders to fire some senior people who tolerated or created the insane schedules. While collisions are not forgivable, putting your subordinates into a position where collisions are inevitable is equally unforgivable.

For the 3 percent and the 2 percent...
Unless it's genuinely a bolt from the blue—totally unexpected—managers usually have a pretty good idea who their knuckleheads are.

As managers transform themselves into leaders, they:

- ✓ quickly get rid of the knuckleheads and the sociopaths, or
- ✓ put the dummies and the malicious into a position where they can do no harm, or
- ✓ train them not to be knuckleheads,[52] if possible.

No system is foolproof for eliminating the 3 percent who can't and the 2 percent who won't. But leaders spend time and process to make sure they can't hurt the enterprise.

Treating the 95 percent like the 2 or 3 percent
When something untoward happens, managers will demand that this mistake never happen again. Their underlying instinct is good; no one wants to make the same mistake twice.

But it's not uncommon for the cure to be worse than the disease.

---

52 You can't train someone out of being a sociopath...

As managers transition to leadership, they resist the urge to fix a problem by treating everyone like a moron or a sociopath.

Leaders resist the urge to fix a problem by treating everyone like a moron or a sociopath

An example from my seagoing days. Submarines in particular and ships in general operate with very high voltage systems, typically 440 volts, designed to turn large pumps and motors. The high voltage is distributed in armored cables coming out of large cabinets called electrical switchboards. Periodically you have to (very carefully) go inside those switchboards for corrective or preventive maintenance.

It's very possible to injure or kill yourself inside those switchboards. Unfortunately, it's happened, and will happen again when people get careless or stupid.

As a direct result of lethal accidents, managers put up big signs with red letters that say, in effect, "Don't do anything stupid inside the switchgear because you might die." Totally unhelpful. Anyone with five minutes onboard knows that switchboards and electricity can kill. Adding another unnecessary layer of bureaucracy likely will not solve the problem—it just makes it more complicated.

In this case, leaders ask:

- ✓ How do I make the switchboard safer?
- ✓ How do I avoid going into the switchboard in the first place?
- ✓ How do I ensure that the people going into the switchboard have the right equipment, have enough rest and training, and are adequately supervised?

Life is tougher if you're not smart, but don't treat everyone like they are not smart!

KEYS TO THE TRANSFORMATION

As managers transition to leaders, they:

- Differentiate between those who want to do well (the great majority) and those who can't or won't.
- Once you determine those who can't or won't:
    - ✓ get rid of them, or
    - ✓ put them into a position where they can do no harm, or
    - ✓ train them, if possible.
- Differentiate between people mistakes and systems/process mistakes.
- Look much harder for systems/process mistakes.
- Make sure that the corrective action is not worse than the mistake.

WHAT AM I GOING TO DO DIFFERENTLY ON MONDAY TO TRANSFORM MYSELF FROM A MANAGER INTO A LEADER?

- Dig deeper into a recent error or mistake. Look for the process problem(s). Be less likely to blame just the people.
- With your senior leadership, identify those in your organization who fall into the 3 percent or 2 percent category, and develop a plan to minimize their harmful impact.

KISS

Origin

KISS, the acronym (not the rock band), has been around for a long time.

The original acronym stood for "Keep it simple, stupid."

I dislike "Keep it simple, stupid" because it denigrates the listener by implying they were stupid.

The concept

KISS=Keep It Simple & Short.

Managers are into the details. But, as managers transition to leaders, they continue to insist on details at the micro-level but now focus on simplifying and abbreviating at the macro-level.

Simplicity is much easier to remember in stressful situations.

Simplicity is also much more fault-tolerant than complexity.

What am I going to do differently on Monday to transform myself from a manager into a leader?

Keep it simple & short—just like this chapter.

Perpetual Optimism Is a Force Multiplier

Origin

Many have said it, since the idea is hardly unique, but it appeared most recently as the final rule of General Colin Powell's informal document, *13 Life Rules for Any Future Leader*.

The concept

This maxim is easy to understand and devilishly difficult to implement.

Approaching every situation, including the most dire, with a smile and a great attitude is so much better for you and your team than the opposite.

No one likes working for or near a grouch. It's that simple.

Smile, always

When he was growing up, my son Ted got tired of me telling him that "Positivity is a force multiplier."

I'm German by birth, and my wife is Scottish by ancestry. Neither nation's general approach to life is known for being expressive, happy-go-lucky, or perpetually optimistic.

Yet between the three of us, when things would get dark, one of us would remind the other two that positivity is a force multiplier. It worked!

At first, I didn't think this aphorism needed a lot of elaboration. Yet it does.

There's a difference between positivity and wishful thinking
Managers understand the facts and the probabilities. We want to know the odds and the details. But humans don't operate on facts and probabilities. They operate on optimism and hope. Leaders provide optimism and hope.

But espousing optimism and hope does not mean lying or exaggerating. Instead, leaders walk a fine line between a positive spin on truth and fantasyland.

> **Leaders provide optimism and hope, but walk a fine line between a positive spin on truth and fantasyland**

There's a difference between genuine positivity and shallow grinning
Be sincere in your optimistic words and demeanor, and if you're not good at it, practice. Avoid insincerity at all costs.

Keep the worry beads hidden
Lothar-Günther Buchheim wrote a novel (later made into the movie *Das Boot*) fictionalizing his experience as a war correspondent on a World War II German submarine on a combat patrol.

The submarine was being depth-charged by British destroyers and was taking a fearful pounding. Everyone was watching the Captain. Was he panicked? Was he nervous? Were they going to make it out of this alive? Buchheim describes the Captain calmly sitting in the corner of the conning tower, reading a book. "Well", thought the crew, "if he's reading a book, it can't be all that bad. Okay, let's go about our business and evade this pesky Brit."

Only much later does the author reveal that the book was upside down, and the Captain wasn't reading anything at all—he was putting on a show of calm in the face of danger. He kept his worry beads hidden. Positivity is a force multiplier.

The glass of water

Managers will tell you exactly how much water is in the glass. Leaders will tell you it's half full, and it tastes good!

KEYS TO THE TRANSFORMATION

As managers transition to leaders, they:

- Learn to be positive in the face of trouble.
- Don't lie or exaggerate.
- Keep their worry beads hidden.

WHAT AM I GOING TO DO DIFFERENTLY ON MONDAY TO TRANSFORM MYSELF FROM A MANAGER INTO A LEADER?

- Pick a problem that worries or troubles you, and deliberately create a positive public perspective on it.

Everything Is Connected to Everything Else

Origin

This is another quote that has been attributed to many but is first ascribed to Leonardo da Vinci.

The full quote: "Develop your senses—especially learn how to see. Realize that everything connects to everything else."

The concept

It's easy to see linear connections. Managers are trained to connect the dots. If A, then B; if B, then C; if C, then D.

Leaders look for non-linear connections. If A and B, then maybe X. If Y, then absolutely not C.

It takes instinct, knowledge, and a finely tuned sense to see and discern the connections that are not obvious to the naked eye.

> **Learn to see and sense what's not visible to the naked eye**

As applied to leadership, these are rarely physical connections. Instead, the maxim refers to political, legal, emotional, informal, and other tenuous, typically invisible, connections.

As managers transform themselves into leaders, they must learn to see and sense what's not visible to the naked eye!

What's a political decision?

Many years ago, a wise leader taught me the definition of a political decision—a decision made in the absence of, or contravention of, the facts.

> **A political decision is a decision made in the absence of, or contravention of, the facts**

Most managers, particularly inexperienced ones, are driven nuts by political decisions. "Damn it, the facts don't support that decision!" is a frequent lament.

Leaders know that the more senior the decision-maker, the stronger the political influences, and the higher the probability of a political decision.

Killing the initiative

In 2014, California voters overwhelmingly rejected a statewide ballot measure, Proposition 46, which sought to weaken the state's Medical Injury Compensation Reform Act (MICRA) by raising the cap on noneconomic[53] damages in medical liability lawsuits to $1.1 million from $250,000.

The proposition was placed on the state ballot by a wealthy individual who had a horrendous personal story of physician malpractice and felt physicians needed to be held more financially accountable.

The initial advertising generated significant early support for Prop. 46—featuring a doctor in a bar drinking, implying that physicians drink before operating and that their bad behavior should be punished financially.

On the surface, that sounded pretty good to the viewer: punish bad behavior by incompetent docs... A lot of voters thought, "Sure, I'll vote for that."

---

53 Essentially, punitive damages.

If approved, Prop. 46 would have had two harmful impacts on the medical community. First, the number of malpractice lawsuits would jump dramatically. Second, physicians' malpractice insurance rates and premiums would double, treble, or more, effectively putting many doctors in small groups or in solo practice out of business.

So far, easy to understand and pretty linear.

Here's where leaders start to separate themselves from managers—it's that ability to look around corners, to see the connections that aren't obvious.

The real winners, if Prop. 46 passed, were the trial lawyers. If Prop. 46 passed, medical malpractice lawsuits, even frivolous ones, would have much higher payouts, therefore much higher contingency fees, and thus would be much more lucrative for the trial bar, leading to more lawsuits (and a subsequent death spiral for doctors).

But there were other influential groups affected if Prop. 46 passed.

- ✓ Patients would be affected since their access to physicians would be reduced.
- ✓ Rural or low-income communities would be affected since fewer physicians could afford to practice in those areas.
- ✓ Hospital systems would be affected since their malpractice insurance would go through the roof.

Prop. 46 was defeated by overwhelming margins because doctors convinced groups that were indirectly yet substantially impacted to contribute against the campaign and vote it down.

They did this by highlighting that Prop. 46 was connected to almost every citizen in California—everything is connected to everything else.

Leaders have to see connections that managers may not!

Seeing around corners

The previous example dealt with seeing unseen but existing connections.

Leaders also have to see connections that don't even exist yet; they have to peer into the future to spot *future* connections!

In her groundbreaking book *Seeing Around Corners*, author Rita McGrath discusses leaders who spot disruptive inflection points (and the associated new connections) developing before they hit.

Managers who think about what has not yet happened, but likely will, are transforming themselves into leaders.

> **Leaders have to peer into the future to spot *future* connections**

Where have all the solos gone?

The lifeblood of any membership organization is the dues that allow the organization to work for the members.

I came on board the Medical Society as CEO in 2001.[54] For the previous 130 years, the backbone of this and many other medical societies was small and solo practices—typically one to five doctors practicing outside of large healthcare systems. The members were conservative, older, and highly independent... and many were failing financially.

The winds of change were blowing and blowing hard. New modes of reimbursement, younger docs, and changing technology all contributed to the slow and then rapid decline of the solo and small group practice.

By studying the membership data and listening far and wide (that is, looking around corners), we realized that SDCMS either had to change or it would die. We had to change our backbone to medium and large groups while not ignoring the solo and small groups.

---

54 My timing was interesting: I reported for work seven days after 9/11 and six weeks before the 2001 anthrax scare (talk about a baptism of fire...).

Managers make sure the present is working smoothly.

Leaders look at what connections the future will bring and ensure their organization is positioned to capture that future.

We quickly adapted to a changing mix of doctors and continued to grow because our leaders could look around corners.

Everything is connected to everything else—and leaders find those connections and exploit them.

KEYS TO THE TRANSFORMATION

As managers transition to leaders, they:

- Spot today's hidden connections.
- Peer into the future to spot the next connections.
- Learn to accept and thrive on political decisions—those made in the absence of, or contravention of, the facts.

WHAT AM I GOING TO DO DIFFERENTLY ON MONDAY TO TRANSFORM MYSELF FROM A MANAGER INTO A LEADER?

- Pick a subset of your world and ask what the current and future unseen connections are or will be.

SECTION 5

LEARNING

My old-fashioned German mother would frequently remind her kids that we had two choices: learn by listening to her words or by getting rapped on the knuckles. And she followed through with that threat!

This section is about managers transforming themselves into leaders by becoming better learners. I picked three aphorisms that help managers to become leaders by learning.

- *Those who do not learn from history are doomed to repeat it.* As managers become leaders, they look wider and deeper. Deeper in terms of history and wider by looking beyond their current situation.

- *Make mistakes. Learn from them. Move on.* Managers grow into leaders by thoughtfully tolerating non-fatal errors, learning from them, and then moving on.
- *Listen.* The more you learn from listening, the better leader you will become.

Those Who Do Not Learn from History Are Doomed to Repeat It

Origin
Many have said something similar, but the most recent attribution is to philosopher George Santayana, who wrote that "Those who cannot remember the past are condemned to repeat it."

The concept
I riffed on Santayana's quote, changing "remember" to "learn from."

Managers remember the obvious lessons of the past. As managers transition to leaders, they push the time horizon farther back and cast a wider net:

- ✓ Leaders go farther back into the past than managers, and
- ✓ Leaders look for lessons learned not just for their organizations but also from similar organizations and sometimes completely different organizations.

Railroads and Microsoft
If you follow the trajectory of Microsoft—from the iconic 1978 photo of rail-thin Bill Gates and his motley crew of 10 to the tril-

lion-dollar behemoth of today—you'd think their explosive growth was a new phenomenon.

But in the early 1870s, the meteoric growth industry of the day was railroading. Fortunes were made (and lost) betting on the exponential growth of this revolutionary mode of transportation.

When the railroads were deemed too big for their britches, accused of exercising monopoly powers, President Teddy Roosevelt campaigned on breaking up the railroad trusts (and did so, famously, in *Northern Securities Co. v. U.S.*).

When Microsoft was deemed too big for their britches, accused of exercising monopoly powers, the government sued them in a multi-decade attempt to break their alleged domination over computer operating systems.

History repeats itself.[55] The French have a wonderful saying[56] that (loosely translated) means the more things change, the more they stay the same.

Leaders are wise to look backward to the future.[57]

> **History repeats itself.**
> **Leaders are wise to look backward to the future**

What's Mickey have to do with a hospital system?
Managers look closely at the history of their organizations and very similar organizations.

Leaders expand the aperture. In addition to looking farther back, they look wider.

In 2007, Sharp HealthCare, the largest healthcare system in San Diego County, won the Malcolm Baldrige National Quality Award, the only recipient in California and one of only five in the nation for that year.

---

55 Karl Marx quipped that "history repeats itself, first as tragedy and then as farce."
56 *Le plus ça change, plus c'est la même chose*, attributed to Jean-Baptiste Alphonse Karr.
57 Interestingly, while the final outcome is yet to be determined, the internet giant Google is, as of this writing, being sued to break up its alleged monopoly. Quoting that famous purveyor of malapropism, Yogi Berra, "It's déjà vu all over again."

The Sharp team consulted with the Disney organization during the long run-up to achieving this award. A manager might ask, "What the heck are we spending time and money to go see Mickey for? We're a hospital, not a theme park!" A leader would argue that hospitals and theme parks are both customer-facing service businesses... and that Disney can teach anyone a lot!

Mike Murphy, Dan Gross, and the Sharp leadership team expanded their lessons-learned aperture well beyond the conventional approach (looking at other hospitals and health systems) and reaped the reward.

Remind me again, how did we do this the last time?
Managers are focused on getting the job done. There's always more to do, so they move on once the job is done.

Leaders insist on taking the time to harvest the lessons learned from any task or evolution.

In the late '80s, I went from Engineer Officer for *Pogy* to the Squadron Engineer, responsible for 10 submarine nuclear power plants.

We started sending out, roughly monthly, a newsletter that encapsulated all the significant lessons learned from all the submarines I worked with. This approach simultaneously spread the information and encouraged the submariners to record the lessons learned. Share the wealth!

As managers transition to leaders, they learn more from the past, learn more from others, and learn more from their mistakes (discussed in the next chapter).

KEYS TO THE TRANSFORMATION

As managers transition to leaders, they:

- Push the lessons-learned horizon farther back in history because history often repeats itself.
- Push the lessons-learned aperture wider by looking outside their industry.
- Aggressively share and record their lessons learned.

WHAT AM I GOING TO DO DIFFERENTLY ON MONDAY TO TRANSFORM MYSELF FROM A MANAGER INTO A LEADER?

- Convene a study group to look at history and industries to identify several specific new ideas.
- Create a process for recording and sharing internal lessons learned.

Make Mistakes.
Learn from
Them.
Move On.

Origin

This saying, or a variation thereon, has been repeated by many authors for many years. However, I was inspired by the long version of the saying in General David Petraeus' informal document, *12 Rules for Living*: "We will all make mistakes. The key is to recognize them and admit them, to learn from them, and to take off the rearview mirrors—drive on and don't make them again."

The concept

Managers avoid risk like the bubonic plague.

Leaders do things differently:

- ✓ They take risks, albeit calculated risks.
- ✓ They bound the risk—they make sure that if things don't work out as desired, the fallout is minimal and not career- or life-ending.
- ✓ They know that risk-taking is necessary for growth.

Managers don't always recognize their mistakes.

Leaders insist on recognizing and admitting their errors.

Managers don't always learn from their mistakes.

Leaders insist on learning from their mistakes; sometimes, learning from a mistake is the major benefit of the error.

Finally, leaders get over their mistakes. You can't drive a car by looking in the rearview mirror!

> **Leaders get over their mistakes**

Make mistakes—carefully

Unlike their World War II elders, modern nuclear submarines have a very delicate front end. The sonar dome—a carefully machined piece of fiberglass—ensures laminar flow over the sonar sphere and thereby makes sure the submarine can hear perfectly.

When a submarine approaches the pier for a landing, the most delicate part of the submarine (the sonar dome) is leading the way. Making a landing is a fundamental skill for any young submarine officer. They have to learn to do it. But, it's considered bad form to crunch your sonar dome. So how do you teach the youngsters to make a successful approach to the pier without dinging your dome?

Clearly, you want to coach and mentor the young officer, but at some point, you have to step back and let them do it. My teachers on *Nautilus* came up with a clever solution. We found a nice quiet spot on Long Island Sound on a calm day, dropped a bunch of buoys over the side to simulate a pier, and then had all the junior officers take turns making an approach on the simulated pier without help or intervention from their seniors. If we screwed up, no harm/no foul.

Managers are risk-averse. Leaders take risks—but bound the risk.

Learn from mistakes

In chapter 22, we discussed learning.

Leaders must insist on reviewing everything that went wrong when mistakes happen.

Every time something goes wrong with an airplane, there's an investigation and a report, even for something relatively minor. If there's pilot or mechanic learning to be had from the mistake, it is promulgated widely.

Managers are risk-averse. Leaders take risks—but bound the risk

So it should be for any organization.

Move on from mistakes

As you transform yourself from manager to leader, you will spend less and less time looking into the rearview mirror.

When my son was growing up, and something went wrong, I would tell him (after we discussed the lessons learned), "Get over it. Get on with it. Move on."

After ensuring the lessons have been learned and corrective action has been taken, leaders move on.

Learn from success

There are many lessons to be learned when things go well. Leaders insist on taking the time to capture the right learnings from success.

In 1905, the Japanese Navy annihilated the Russian fleet at the Battle of Tsushima, and brought a swift end to the Russo-Japanese War. Superior Japanese technology, training, and leadership brought about this stunning victory. But the Japanese crucially misread the lessons of Tsushima at the start of World War II. They incorrectly assumed that the United States, handed a singular knockout blow like Pearl Harbor, would fold their cards, as did the Russians, and accede to Japanese demands. Anyone who understood America knew that, unlike Imperial Russia, the American people would never accept the results of Pearl Harbor, and that the industrial might of America would eventually overwhelm Japan.

Learning the wrong lessons from success can be just as hazardous as not learning the lessons from failure.

KEYS TO THE TRANSFORMATION

As managers transition to leaders, they:

- Take risks, albeit calculated ones.
- Bound the risk: they make sure that if things don't work out as desired, the fallout is minimal and not career- or life-ending.
- Learn from failure.
- Learn the right lessons from success.
- Know that risk-taking is necessary for growth.

WHAT AM I GOING TO DO DIFFERENTLY ON MONDAY TO TRANSFORM MYSELF FROM A MANAGER INTO A LEADER?

- Pick an event or evolution where you will encourage and tolerate risk-taking and mistakes.

Listen

Origin
There are thousands of aphorisms about listening.

The concept
Unless they are dictators, every leader has been told, emphatically, "Listen."

Managers, most of them, are not bad listeners. However, as they transform themselves into leaders, they must become great listeners.

The key to effective listening is recognizing that leaders must listen to many voices—their own as well as those of others, including friends, enemies, and people who don't think as they do.

And they must hear what didn't get said. | **Hear what didn't get said**

Listen to yourself (the voice within)
I cannot overemphasize learning to listen to your own voice. You likely got to your position because you have a robust set of ethics and values coupled with a strong inner compass. Combine that

inner compass with the ability to see that something is a-kilter where others don't, and you have a great advisor—yourself.

But you have to learn to trust yourself and listen to yourself.

Listen to those who don't think as you do

Get outside your comfort zone. Reach out to find people who don't think like you— those with different backgrounds and those who add diversity to your counsel.

> **Reach out to find people who don't think like you**

I served on the board of a not-for-profit health Information Technology (IT) organization that provided electronic health record interoperability for San Diego County.

I was the outsider. The total of my health IT technical knowledge would fit on the head of a pin. But, I consistently asked the "dumb question"[58]—a question that all the experts had a pat answer to. Upon deeper probing and the application of common sense, it turned out that the answer(s) to the ostensibly dumb questions were not so clear or so obvious.

If you surround yourself with "yes" people, you run the risk of running around clueless, as in the fable of the Emperor's New Clothes.

Groupthink

Groupthink can be literally and figuratively deadly.

The *Challenger* space shuttle explosion in 1986 was due to the failure of the rocket booster seals during cold weather. The middle-level engineers knew the dangers of launching the shuttle in cold weather. Unfortunately, the NASA seniors ignored them.

---

58 The questions were not dumb, but by self-deprecating, I was able to ask them without hurting feelings.

Three fundamentals were at work:

- ✓ leaders had not encouraged subordinates to speak up, *and*
- ✓ leaders had not been willing to listen to what subordinates had to say, *and*
- ✓ subordinates did not dare to disagree emphatically with the deadly decision.

As managers transition to leaders, they create a culture of speaking up and listening to message(s) they perhaps don't want to hear.

> **Create a culture of speaking up and listening**

Listen to what didn't get said

Peter Drucker, a renowned management consultant, famously stated, "The most important thing in communication is hearing what isn't said."

Listening to the silence is one of the most difficult and valuable traits of a leader.

One of my role models at SDCMS was famously opaque with criticism. After a while, you learned to listen for elliptic phrases from him. We who knew him well would kid that when he asked if you knew the dates for the next sale at Nordstrom, he was really telling you that you needed to buff up your wardrobe.

But he at least would say *something*. Many in your entourage will say *nothing*.

Transforming yourself into a leader requires searching for the unsaid and getting those unsaid words out into the open.

Let's say the team you lead just completed a very high-visibility project. You and the team thought everyone did a great job under intense pressure.

However, at the local watering hole, none of your peers, as would be expected by social norms, is effusively congratulatory about the project. Instead, surprisingly to you, they are a tad standoffish.

Managers would enthuse and brag about the project, but leaders would wonder why none of their peers was enthused.

In this example, now would be an excellent time to speak with one of your trusted peers and find out why everyone is giving you the cold shoulder.

Don't shoot the messenger

I had a tough time on my second ship. I had to be hard-nosed, but carried it too far. I had a classmate, a terrific officer, who happened to also work for me. One day he invited me out to lunch off the ship. Rather tactfully, he told me how I was messing up.

I was not receptive. I had an explanation for everything and, to my detriment, ignored his message. I had, figuratively, shot the messenger.

When you ignore or deprecate the messenger, they won't come back to you, and the word will quickly get out, and then no other messengers will come to you. A leader isolated from bad news is in serious trouble.

> **Don't ever, ever, ever, ever shoot or ignore the messenger**

It took me a while to recover that trust.

Don't ever, ever, ever, ever shoot or ignore the messenger—the career you save may be your own!

Create a culture of speaking up

Reward the messenger when they bring you bad news. Thank them effusively in public and private.

What I should have done is gathered my team, asked my classmate to point out the issues of concern, thanked him, and then asked for my team to tell me what else I could improve on.

It's not hard, but it requires inner strength. Listen. To yourself. To others. To those who don't think like you. To what didn't get said. Reward the messenger, never punish them.

KEYS TO THE TRANSFORMATION

As managers transition to leaders, they:

- Listen to themselves.
- Listen to those who don't think as they do.
- Listen to those who disagree with them.
- Listen for what didn't get said.
- Create a culture of speaking up.

WHAT AM I GOING TO DO DIFFERENTLY ON MONDAY TO TRANSFORM MYSELF FROM A MANAGER INTO A LEADER?

- Create a "kitchen cabinet" of trusted peers who are willing and able to tell you the uncomfortable truths.
- Set up a process where you proactively seek out team members to tell you the uncomfortable truths.

SECTION 6

CARING

Managers are problem-solvers, rightly focused on accomplishing tasks.

As managers transition to leaders, they recognize that they need to care for their teams and care for themselves to accomplish the amazing.

I picked two aphorisms about caring:

- *Leaders eat last.* This is a metaphor that reflects that the leader must care for their team.
- *Life is short, eat dessert first.* It's not enough to take care of your people—you also have to take care of yourself.

Leaders Eat Last

Origin

"Leaders eating last" is a relatively recent articulation[59] in the leadership literature but is a well-established concept for elite militaries.

The concept

Every young Marine officer is taught that they eat after their troops. It's not a matter of gastronomy. It's the symbolic recognition that you cannot do your job without your people, and your people cannot do their job unless they are fed (literally as well as figuratively).

"Leader eats last" is a metaphor that says leaders ensure that their people are taken care of.

Taking care of your people is not conceptually challenging. In keeping with KISS, this will be a short chapter.

But caring has to come from the heart. If you're saying nice words but not following up with deeds, your people will smell hypocrisy, and you will quickly lose their trust and confidence.

---

59 The topic is delved into fully in the book *Leaders Eat Last* by Simon Sinek

23 TRUTHS THAT TRANSFORM MANAGERS INTO LEADERS

Leaders pitch in

Let's say you are the manager of a 15-person unit tasked with writing an elaborate budget proposal under intense time pressure.

An inexperienced manager would assign their team the task, go home, and yell at the team when they fall behind.

An experienced manager would give detailed instructions from their perch in their 28th-floor aerie and stay out of their team's way.

A leader would:

- ✓ Create a temporary office near the team—to be close but not too close.
- ✓ Assign some difficult portions of the task to themselves.
- ✓ Be the first to show up and last to leave.
- ✓ Ensure that all the personal needs (e.g., food, time for a shower or a workout, admin support, etc.) are taken care of.
- ✓ Finally, and most importantly, the leader would pay close attention to the team's morale and do whatever it takes to keep the group engaged in the task at hand.

Leaders eat last. Leaders take care of their people. Leaders care for their people from the heart.

KEYS TO THE TRANSFORMATION

As managers transition to leaders, they:

- Take care of all the needs of their people.
- Are genuine about that care.

WHAT ARE YOU GOING TO DO DIFFERENTLY ON MONDAY TO TRANSFORM YOURSELF FROM A MANAGER TO A LEADER?

- For a current project, find out whether your people have what they need to do the work you assigned.

Life Is Short, Eat Dessert First!

Origin

This quote is attributed to French pastry chef Jacques Torres.

The concept

While Torres may be referring to a literal dessert, I interpret this in the same vein as *carpe diem*, the Latin phrase interpreted as "seize the day."[60]

Management is hard, but leadership is harder.

As you transform yourself into a leader, the demands on your time, energy, and emotions will ramp up dramatically.

> **Management is hard, but leadership is harder. You have to take care of yourself**

You have to take care of yourself, and you have to keep the big picture in mind: that life is indeed short, and you don't want to miss out on dessert—I never pass it up!

---

60 Literally, "pluck the day." The words are actually part of a longer phrase attributed to the Roman writer Horace, *Carpe diem, quam minimum credula postero*, which is often translated as "Seize the day, put very little trust in tomorrow (the future)."

Put your oxygen mask on first

You've heard this phrase every time you prepared for takeoff: "In the event of a sudden drop in cabin pressure, an oxygen mask will drop from above. Secure your own mask first before assisting others."

You have to take care of yourself before you take care of others.

I served on active duty for more than 22 years. Service members are entitled to 30 days of paid vacation a year, but you cannot accumulate more than 60 days. If you didn't use it, you lost it. Many of my submarine compatriots, an incredibly hardworking and dedicated bunch, made it a badge of honor to constantly lose accrued leave. For me, the opposite was true. When I was not on holiday, I worked insanely hard. But I never lost a single day of leave—I used every last day of vacation!

One of the early pieces of advice I got from Frank Stewart, my first department head, was, "If you don't have anything to do, don't do it here [at work]."

My message to leaders (and managers) is simple: take care of yourself—take time off when you can.

There is no rewind button on life

There is no do-over. You can't get back time or the moments in life that make it unique. Be dedicated, yes, but don't miss the important things, or the mundane things, in life.

Go to your kid's volleyball game. Have dinner with your spouse with the cell phones in the other room. Take the time in the middle of the day to run or get outside and enjoy the breeze or the sunshine or the rain.

Good job, Mommy

Our son, Ted, was born when we were both 43, so we were a tad more mature when dealing with the challenges of child-rearing. Cathy did a great job in his first years of life, always rewarding him verbally when he did something well. And when he didn't do it perfectly, she dwelt not on the imperfection but rather on that portion done well.

One day when our son was in grade school, Cathy was verbally deprecating herself for some imagined fault. Ted, overhearing this, chimed in with, "No, Mommy, you did a good job!" Out of the mouths of babes....

> **Be your best critic but also your best advocate**

The episode served as a powerful reminder that you have to be introspective, yes, but also look for what you did well.

Be your best critic but also your best advocate.

Remind yourself that you are making a tangible positive difference in people's lives—at work and at home.

It's a marathon, not a sprint—but go run!

Leadership, even for short periods, is grueling. Eat well, exercise, and get sleep. You can't keep up a killer pace forever. If your endurance sags, so will the performance of your team.

One of the things I teach future leaders is to program into the daily schedule some "me time," whether for yoga, exercise, meditation, or anything else that centers you.

Rain or shine for almost 45 years, I ran during most of my lunch breaks. Knowing full well the intense stress I was under as Engineer Officer, my skipper on *Pogy* would routinely come down to my stateroom and "invite" me to go running. I protested mightily that I had a full inbox and lots to do. "Lace up your shoes, Engineer," said the skipper. We would squeeze off a quick three or five miles, and I went back to work refreshed for another half day. It kept me sane and healthy.

Carpe diem, put your oxygen mask on first, and go run!

And do the same for your people

In today's ultracompetitive world, many people assume it's a badge of honor to work more hours, spend more weekend days working, and take less vacation.

Poppycock! You know better. Insist that your people work hard but not 26 hours a day, tell them to go home on weekends, and insist they take a vacation.

And if it's their birthday or their wedding anniversary—lock out their computer and tell them to go out to dinner with their spouse.

Managers count hours. Leaders count results. Life is short—eat dessert first.

KEYS TO THE TRANSFORMATION

As managers transition to leaders, they:

- Learn to take care of themselves first.
- Program "me time" into their daily schedule.
- Take the time to say nice things to themselves.
- Eat well, exercise, and get sleep.

WHAT AM I GOING TO DO DIFFERENTLY ON MONDAY TO TRANSFORM MYSELF FROM A MANAGER INTO A LEADER?

- Find something nice to say to yourself about something great you did this week.
- Fence at least 30 minutes at work every day that only your spouse or significant other may interrupt.

SECTION 7

CASE STUDIES

Theory is dry, but stories bring ideas to life.

I wanted to operationalize the *23 Truths That Transform Managers into Leaders* by dint of these three fictional (yet reality-based) examples.

Enjoy the stories, and as you read them, constantly ask yourself, "What would I do differently?"

Case Study #1 – Little Cog in a Big Wheel

The Situation

Sasha is a millennial who grew up in rural Iowa, the only child of university professors at Grinnell University, a highly select but very small institute. He received a full scholarship to, and graduated with honors from, Dartmouth College[61] five years ago with a double major in Computer Sciences and Economics.

Sasha turned down several lucrative offers from high-tech Silicon Valley firms and prestigious consulting companies.

He chose to work for FeedLots, the largest not-for-profit in Des Moines, focused on addressing widespread hunger among the rural disadvantaged in the Midwest.

FeedLots is mission-driven with a great culture and a dynamic young female CEO, Frida, who came from a disadvantaged rural background. She also graduated from Dartmouth, 10 years before Sasha, and recruited Sasha after meeting him at an alumni mixer.

---

61 Dartmouth College is the most rural of the Ivy League and the second oldest—and, says the proud father, the alma mater of my son.

Sasha has excelled as the manager of FeedLots' 10 person IT department. He is working on an Executive MBA at night and wants to move up to a more senior position as a Vice President of Operations (VP-Ops) when the incumbent retires in a couple of years.

Big Picture

Sasha is an effective manager. Frida has told him, and his people have told him.

Yet, he is floundering in making the transition from manager to leader.

There's no switch or software or hardware that he can find to transform himself. While there are books and courses galore, most of them are too theoretical and not pragmatic enough.

Focusing

Sasha knows he needs a plan, a framework, a protocol.

He decides to sit down with Frida for a long, off-campus lunch. He has two fundamental questions for her:

- ✓ Where should I be going in my leadership journey?
- ✓ How do you suggest I get there?

He takes copious notes from the extended conversation.

Next, he looks for at least one and hopefully two mentors in the Des Moines business community, the local Dartmouth alumni club, or the local Rotary or Lions club. Then he does the same thing: a long lunch with the same two fundamental questions.

After one or two months, Sasha has created a rough outline for a path to leadership.

If you don't know where you're going, any road will get you there. Sasha now knows where he is going.

CASE STUDY #1 – LITTLE COG IN A BIG WHEEL

From his detailed discussions with Frida and his plan, Sasha identifies his main thing: to be promoted to the "C" suite as VP-Ops at FeedLots in one to three years.

He keeps this "main thing" private, known only to his spouse and Frida—who encouraged him to follow that path.[62]

While there are many demands on his time, Sasha spends at least an hour every month with Frida to review his progress. The preparations for those recurring meetings force him to focus on the steps toward his "main thing."

But there is more. Sasha realizes that achieving VP-Ops is not a sure thing. So he starts quietly networking with out-of-town headhunters to raise his profile and see whether there are other possibilities.

In addition, he expands his perspective by seeking out best practices both for his IT shop and the whole operations department. He knows that it will be good for himself and his team to look farther and wider.

Leading

Sasha takes a new approach to his responsibilities. He accepts and then embraces that *everything* IT is his responsibility. While he gives credit to his team, he accepts the faults and errors. However, before taking that step, he makes sure his direct boss, Sam, the current VP-Ops, and Frida know that he will be changing his language to reflect his change in thinking. Sasha places an antique brass "The Buck Stops Here" plaque on his desk, similar to President Truman's. He sends an email to all the VPs with his cell number and invites them to call him whenever there's a problem.

On the following several major projects, Sasha decides to take a more proactive role—carefully. He does not want to micromanage, but he does want to be visibly engaged in the hard work. Sasha makes it a point to be present during the grueling

---
62 Sasha has to be cautious not to appear too aggressive; there is often blowback to naked ambition.

final phases of the next project. He finds a way to be helpful without becoming too involved in the easy stuff.

When the team hits a roadblock because of an incompetent industry partner, Sasha, with Frida and Sam's blessing, fires that partner. When the team needs an additional piece of expensive hardware, Sasha maxes his corporate account and obtains what's required. He uses his power.

Actioning

Sasha also completely changes his perspective on meetings. Rather than have long discussions with nebulous endpoints, he insists that his team identify specific and measurable actions and deliverables for each portion of the meeting. He puts up a big sign in his office, "What are you going to do differently on Monday?" His team quickly gets the message, and productivity increases. And the meetings are *shorter*!

Problems are inevitable, but this one is a doozy! A fire in the server farm that FeedLots uses, despite all the precautions, wipes out the primary data hub for the organization. Of course, they have a backup, but it looks corrupted. C-suite panic sets in. What to do? Sasha convenes an emergency meeting of the IT team. He challenges them to come up with creative solutions—to improvise. His quietest and most withdrawn tech comes up with an ingenious solution, which will require the entire FeedLots system to shut down for eight hours. But there are no viable alternatives. Sasha authorizes the shutdown and then briefs Frida. The fix, while not perfect, gets FeedLots back online.

Sasha does two things immediately. First, with Frida at his side, he publicly recognizes the tech and hands them a sizable check in recognition of their ingenuity. Second, as soon as the IT system is stable, Sasha convenes a post-mortem to determine the double failure's root cause.

More importantly, he authorizes a deep dive by an outside consultant to identify *all* the possible future failure points; he conducts a pre-mortem and invites representatives from all the other C-suite direct reports to make it maximally inclusive.

Sasha initiates a monthly IT disaster drill to rehearse the IT team responses once they have identified the top five failure points with the greatest potential harm. He takes pains to make sure the C-suite is aware of the risk, the exercise, and IT's role in mitigating the crisis.

Philosophizing

Eighteen months into his plan to become VP-Ops, Sasha hits a wall.

Because of the COVID pandemic and the attendant economic issues, FeedLots has to reduce the budget by more than 25 percent. The IT system and department are not immune and take an across-the-board cut in personnel and operating funds. Capital improvements are zeroed out.

His team is frustrated by personnel losses and future funding uncertainty. Sasha meets individually with his team members and asks them to focus on the art of the possible—what *can* they do, knowing full well what they can't do.

Sasha, in group meetings, doesn't sugarcoat the problems. He answers every question from his team honestly but focuses, where possible, on solutions, not problems. As a result, while still stressed, the IT team at least has a plan to deal with the personal and professional stressors.

When offered the choice to take a salary cut or lose one of his most conscientious but financially stressed junior people, Sasha takes the salary cut to keep his team together. He knows it's the right thing to do!

Six months into the pandemic, his team is exhausted. They have been supporting the mission—which has ballooned as a result of the crisis—with significantly fewer resources. Kara, one of his best team members, makes an incredibly dumb mistake on the midnight shift.⁶³ Sasha immediately convenes a critique to determine the cause and the corrective action.

Luckily, the corrective action is relatively mild—only two hours of data (from midnight to 2 am) are lost, and that data can be manually recreated.

But Sasha is faced with a difficult choice. What to do with Kara?

The tough call is to decide whether this was a one-off (all of us make mistakes) or a systemic issue. Does Kara belong in the 3 percent (incompetents) or the 2 percent (sociopaths)? With the concurrence of Sam, he quickly concludes that the real problem was not Kara but the overwhelming working hours that Kara had assumed to cover for some of the team who had pandemic-related family issues. Kara was not the problem, the system was the problem. Sasha takes immediate proactive steps to ensure exhaustion is not routine and sits down with every team member to reiterate that the team must work together to mitigate fatigue.

Learning

Sasha also knows that innovation rules. He creates a no-fault innovation program. Everyone is allowed a very small (given the fiscal realities) budget of time and money to try something new and crazy—after selling Sasha on it and making sure the risk is bounded.

A small group comes up with a brilliant but unorthodox way to reduce the data site costs by safely un-duplicating records storage. Sasha listens and implements the innovative plan, and the tangible savings are plowed back into salaries to mitigate the impact of the pandemic.

---

63 The midshift, usually between midnight and 6 am, is notorious for sourcing a preponderance of major mistakes. People are sleep deprived or their sleep pattern is off, there is less supervision, and there are usually fewer people. The Chernobyl accident, although it had many causes, happened on the midwatch for precisely those reasons.

Caring

Instinctively, Sasha wants to work harder and longer. Counterintuitively, he doesn't. He realizes that he can spend every waking hour working, but that's a fool's errand in both the medium- and long-term.

He creates white space on his calendar for "alone, door shut" time and incorporates exercise into his daily routine. He knows he has to care for himself just as much as he cares for his people.

Finally, he has a series of long talks with his spouse, who also works in a demanding job.

They create a personal strategic plan that factors in their plans to start a family. They make a firm commitment to each other to not let their jobs define or overwhelm them.

So, what would you do differently?

Take a look at the list of the 23 truths below, and ask yourself, "What else could Sasha do?"

Focusing

- If you don't know where you're going, any road will get you there.
- Make the main thing the main thing.
- What you see depends on where you stand.

Leading

- The buck stops here.
- Lead from the front.
- May the force be with you.

Actioning

- What are you going to do differently on Monday?
- Plans are nothing, planning is everything.
- Improvise, adapt, and overcome.
- It is better to sweat in peace than bleed in war.
- Why? Why? Why? Why? Why? Why?

Philosophizing
- Do what you can, with what you've got, where you are at.
- Nothing hard is ever easy.
- What's the right thing to do here?
- Life is tough, but it's tougher if you're not smart.
- KISS
- Perpetual optimism is a force multiplier.
- Everything is connected to everything else.

Learning
- Those who do not learn from history are doomed to repeat it.
- Make mistakes. Learn from them. Move on.
- Listen.

Caring
- Leaders eat last.
- Life is short, eat dessert first!

Case Study #2 - Big Cog in a Little Wheel

The Situation

Margaret is a Gen-X widow with two teenagers at home. She is a child of immigrants, and English is her second language. She graduated from Cal State Long Beach 20 years ago, obtained her law degree at night at a local law school, and made partner at a small boutique law firm in Los Angeles by dint of incredibly hard work and exceptional courtroom results.

The firm's Managing Partner, Pascale, has made it clear that she expects Margaret to take over as Managing Partner[64] when Pascale retires in about three years. Margaret is enthusiastic about the prospect, but with a caveat: her focus on litigation and the firm's small size has precluded her from any management or leadership experience.

Margaret is deeply concerned about preparing herself for the sharp increase in the Managing Partner's non-legal responsibilities.

---

64 Managing Partner is a really a misnomer. While it certainly requires management, it is much more leading than managing. Most firms, even small ones, have a full-time non-lawyer Chief Operating Officer to do the preponderance of the managing. The Managing Partner is really the leader of the law firm.

The Big Picture

Margaret's big picture is different from Sasha's—she has no managerial experience at all. However, with the support of the current Managing Partner, her elevation to Managing Partner in three years is pretty close to a sure thing.

Her challenge is that she knows nothing at all about managing (never mind leading). So, she needs a crash course in both managing and leading.

Focusing

Margaret and Pascale sit down for a long morning with an executive coach to map out a three-year strategy for the successful handoff of the Managing Partner position from Pascale to Margaret. They develop a detailed plan with frequent feedback.

In addition to meeting monthly with her executive coach, Margaret enrolls in a part-time micro-MBA program at a prestigious local university, paid for by the firm and with work time allocated to the course.

There are two major temporal roadblocks: Margaret's family and her legal work. You can buy almost anything except more time. But you can buy services that will help you find more time.

On the home front, Margaret sits down with each of her kids, lays out the challenge(s), and asks for their help to balance her pursuit of leadership with the parental obligations of two teenagers approaching college.

On the work front, Margaret and Pascale sit down with each of the other seven partners to lay out the plan and ask for their support. Because it's a small, tight-knit group of partners, there is none of the usual politicking and posturing.[65]

Margaret appreciates that there are three "main things" and that there are stressors between them.[66]

---

[65] I recognize that such a peaceful transition of power is less and less likely as a firm grows larger, but the chapter is not about politics but about transitioning to leadership.

[66] See the discussion related to the maxim "Nothing hard is ever easy" (chapter 16).

- ✓ On a personal level, the main thing is to keep her family thriving as a single parent.
- ✓ On an individual professional level, the main thing is learning how to be a manager and a leader, thereby preparing herself to be Managing Partner.
- ✓ On a collective professional level, the main thing is to keep the small firm working together and growing.

Balancing the three "main things," one for each of her roles, will be a constant challenge. There will be no one correct answer, but there will be many wrong answers, such as:

- ✓ Overweighting work versus family (the classic work-life imbalance)
- ✓ Overweighting either individual professional responsibilities or collective professional responsibilities, to the detriment of the other

Margaret needs to, at least monthly, check in with each counterpart(s) in her three roles. Constant feedback and open communications are the best tools to balance the "main things" of the various roles.

She and her counterpart(s) need to accept that there will be brief periods of imbalance and that during those periods, everyone together must find ways to mitigate the impacts.

Leading

When you're trying a case, there's only one lead attorney, so Margaret has a visceral understanding of "the buck stops here" and "lead from the front." The transition to embracing responsibility and leading from the front will not be hard for Margaret.

What will be novel to her is the idea of having and using power. Like all leaders of talented people, the Managing Partner has an obligation to tread carefully—but eventually, Managing Partners have to make choices. Margaret needs to learn and accept that not every choice in a consensual leadership position will be popular; her decisions need to be carefully made and then proven correct. But she has to accept the scepter and orb of power and then wield them carefully.[67]

Actioning

Margaret is used to translating words into action. You don't excel in the courtroom by dithering or not being able to move forward. The hard part is now translating that personal bent to action to a collective bent to action. Margaret needs to start asking others, "What are you going to do differently on Monday?" instead of just herself. This transition is surprisingly hard for many!

Likewise, any trial attorney knows that surprises happen in court. If you can't improvise and adapt, you will fail. Like her ability to translate words into action, Margaret has demonstrated this skill as an individual attorney, but now she has to engender that same adaptability in others.

Likewise, the skills of asking why and planning. The biggest challenge in actioning is not knowing *how*—Margaret does—but helping her subordinates and partners behave the same way. She has to teach and demonstrate actioning.

Philosophizing

Every leader has a leadership style, which they need to articulate to themselves and their team. Margaret needs to write down her leadership philosophy and hold herself accountable to it.

And she must be willing to modify that philosophy as her experience in leadership grows.[68]

---

[67] The heavily bejeweled scepter and orb are part of the coronation regalia of the English king or queen and are symbolic of the monarch's power.

[68] As previously mentioned, I have attached my CEO's philosophy statement as appendix 4—and invite you to plagiarize!

Learning

The three-year transition from courtroom to manager to leader will have stumbles. Margaret needs to accept that. Pascale needs to accept that. And her fellow partners need to accept that.

Using her executive coach and MBA classmates, Margaret needs to find several lawyers who have experienced a similar transition from the courtroom to the corner office. She should regularly meet with those who have trod the same path to learn from their mistakes and their successes.

Risk-taking as a leader is a balancing act between the reward and the potential downside. Margaret has to translate the return-on-investment thinking she displayed in the courtroom to the boardroom. Take some risk, but not too much risk, and certainly no unbounded risk.

Finally, and perhaps most importantly, she must listen to her partners and her kids. She needs to regularly meet individually with each of her fellow partners. Get their feedback, listen carefully both to what is said and what is not said, and act on their concerns. She needs their formal and informal support. Likewise with her children. She should regularly take each teenager out on a "date night" and probe about how it's going and what could be done better.[69]

Caring

Caring for herself will be one of the biggest challenges for Margaret in the transition to leadership. The impulse will be to work harder and longer, and spend as little time on self and family as possible.

The solution is effective delegation.[70] Margaret should hire a top-notch executive assistant and ask them to relieve her of as much of her routine tasks as possible. She needs to structure

---

[69] Parents of teenagers know that this is much easier said than done.
[70] I spend an entire book, *7 Roles Great Leaders Don't Delegate,* on how to manage the delegation process effectively.

her day so there is built-in self-time. And she needs to ruthlessly guard her personal time.

The transformation from lawyer to manager to leader requires Margaret to take a similarly thoughtful approach to her team. It's easy to mandate more—more work, more time at the office, more, more, more... But rather than become a caricature of a bad boss, she needs to emphasize smart work, not more work.

So, what would you do differently?

Take a look at the list of the 23 truths below, and ask yourself, "What else could Margaret do?"

Focusing
- If you don't know where you're going, any road will get you there.
- Make the main thing the main thing.
- What you see depends on where you stand.

Leading
- The buck stops here.
- Lead from the front.
- May the force be with you.

Actioning
- What are you going to do differently on Monday?
- Plans are nothing, planning is everything.
- Improvise, adapt, and overcome.
- It is better to sweat in peace than bleed in war.
- Why? Why? Why? Why? Why?

Philosophizing
- Do what you can, with what you've got, where you are at.
- Nothing hard is ever easy.
- What's the right thing to do here?
- Life is tough, but it's tougher if you're not smart.

- KISS
- Perpetual optimism is a force multiplier.
- Everything is connected to everything else.

Learning
- Those who do not learn from history are doomed to repeat it.
- Make mistakes. Learn from them. Move on.
- Listen.

Caring
- Leaders eat last.
- Life is short, eat dessert first!

Case Study #3 - Janus

The Situation

Dr. Jorge Castanudo is a 33-year-old scientist who graduated Phi Beta Kappa from Stanford and earned a PhD in molecular biochemistry from CalTech. He is on the fast track to national and international honors based on his groundbreaking research in recombinant DNA.

Shortly after receiving his doctorate, Jorge crowd-funded a biotech startup to commercialize recombinant DNA technologies with two other recent CalTech PhDs. Series A[71] funding followed shortly. Three patent applications were fast-tracked during the COVID pandemic and were recently approved.

He married one of the other co-founders, Karin Hasselbeck, MD/PhD. The couple has three-year-old twins. They have a rock-solid personal and professional relationship.

---

71 Series A funding follows initial seed capital, generally bringing in investments in the tens of millions of dollars. A startup will generally draw this level of financing only after it has demonstrated a viable business model with strong growth potential.

The other co-founder, Dr. Jim Epstein, died 15 months ago in a tragic bicycle accident. Jim was highly organized and was the organizational backbone for the trio.

Their company, Acrux,[72] is growing exponentially and recently received $20 million in Series A funding.

Jorge is Chief Executive Officer (CEO), and Karin is the Chief Medical Officer (CMO).

Jorge and Karin are cheerful, bright, thoughtful, and personable. Jorge is an inspirational and visionary leader; his team would follow him anywhere.

He is a brilliant scientist and a visionary—and he hates anything associated with management or making the trains run on time. To Jorge, any time spent on the mundane tasks of running Acrux is wasted time. In the vernacular, Jorge couldn't organize a one-car funeral procession.

The venture capitalists (VCs) who provided Series A funding to Acrux insisted that Jorge hire a highly experienced Chief Operating Officer (COO), essentially, Jorge's right-hand person. Jorge fully supported that decision because he is self-aware and knows his weakness.

Beth Kennedy, both his and the VCs' top choice for COO, graduated from the Naval Academy 16 years ago and was highly decorated flying Cobra attack helicopters in combat. After leaving the Marines a decade ago, she obtained a Harvard MBA and started her career in biotech. She is dynamic, experienced, and widely respected.

Jorge and Beth get along famously. They understand and respect each other. Their offices are side by side, with an interior door between them. They frequently socialize with Karin and Jamir, Beth's spouse.

---

72 Acrux is one of the four stars in the Southern Cross, an easily identified and culturally significant stellar formation visible in the Southern Hemisphere.

Jorge and Beth have cleanly divided Acrux's responsibilities. Jorge is the visionary leader and co-chief scientist with Karin, while Beth runs everything.

Acrux has a flagship product that uses recombinant DNA to address diabetes.

Jorge and his science team are making fantastic progress toward developing three other products that use the same technology to address other diseases.

The Big Picture
Acrux has a brilliant leader, Jorge, and a brilliant manager, Beth.

Jorge, by choice, is completely disconnected from management. He stepped into leadership without ever passing through management.

Contrast this with Margaret in the previous case study, who needed to learn management and leadership simultaneously.

Contrast this with Sasha in the first case study, who has mastered management and then needed to transition to leadership.

This case study is about merging and aligning the skill sets of two people—a superb manager and a superb leader.

Janus, the Roman deity famous for having two faces looking in opposite directions but one mind, should become the model for Jorge and Beth.

They have split the management and leadership roles, but they both need to learn from each other and work together to achieve results for Acrux.

The interior door that connects their offices is both real and metaphorical.

Focusing
Jorge is spending almost all his time in the lab. He is focused on the next big thing(s).

After an initial burst of success with their flagship product, most startups hit a wall because they either have no plans or too many diffuse plans beyond the next round of funding. Acrux needs a post-startup vision and strategic plan. They need a roadmap to stable growth.

But the "main thing" Jorge is energized by is rapidly expanding the product line with new and innovative products. On the other hand, Beth is concerned about burning through cash too quickly by spending on too many things at once.

Beth needs to temper Jorge's exponential growth goals with reality. Jorge has to push Beth into not being excessively conservative. Together they should reach out to Karin for her views. Then, they need to sell the VCs on their "main thing." But what is most important is that everyone agrees on a "main thing."

Once Jorge and Beth agree on the "main thing," they should create a vision and strategies that lead to the next step in the company's growth.

Leading

There is a risk with splitting the manager and leader roles, particularly if the leader has no clue about management. If Beth and Jorge do not work closely together, chaos could ensue. In the vernacular, there can never be any daylight between them.

Where does the buck stop? Who is ultimately responsible? Jorge has to embrace that he is the CEO—he cannot delegate responsibility to Beth. Authority yes, responsibility no.

On the other hand, Beth has to accept that Jorge is the CEO. She needs to make her case for a decision, but it's her role to implement it once made. She can never second-guess or doubt once the decision is made. Luckily for Acrux, her time in the Marines taught her that lesson well.

But who will be the face of the company? How will Jorge lead from the front? This is a delicate balancing act because Jorge is the scientific genius behind Acrux, yet absent Beth's organizational skills, Acrux will fail. Beth will need to be close by whenever

Jorge is on a literal or figurative podium. Jorge needs to encourage Beth to step forward when he is in unknown waters.

Actioning

Because Beth is such a strong COO, actioning will go well.

Yet as Acrux grows, Jorge cannot afford to remain ignorant of actioning. He needs to improve his ability to act outside the lab, so Beth should gently mentor Jorge to improve his actioning outside the lab.

Likewise, Jorge should periodically take Beth into the lab to educate her on the science and how things get done in the lab. This will strengthen her ability to make decisions that impact the lab.

Beth and Jorge need to draw clear decision-making boundaries so that each understands the other's decision space.

What worked for a small and agile Acrux will not necessarily work for a larger and less nimble Acrux. There will be a constant tug of war between Jorge's style as the improviser/adapter and Beth's style as the process-driven and deliberate voice for minimizing risk. Both have to accept that that is normal, and in fact, those differences in style should encourage productive discussions.

Every so often, under Karin's watchful eye, Jorge and Beth should *privately* swap roles: let Jorge play-act that he is COO and let Beth simulate being CEO. That will create a terrific learning environment for both and will likely improve decision-making.

Philosophizing

The top three at Acrux (Jorge, Beth, and Karin) are great people.[73] They are perpetual optimists.

Yet challenges appear.

Brewster, Jorge's college roommate, is miserable as the chief scientist at a rival company. One Friday evening, just before heading out to dinner with their spouses, Jorge drops into Beth's

---

[73] Regretfully, this is rarely so. The employees at Acrux should count themselves lucky.

office and announces that he will make an offer to Brewster to join Acrux.

Beth is inwardly appalled. Hiring Brewster could create major legal and ethical problems. How to steer Acrux away from this minefield? After engaging outside counsel, chatting with a fellow COO in her network, and a phone call with the head of the VCs who funded Acrux, she is placed in the unenviable position of telling Jorge that hiring Brewster is a non-starter. She asks Jorge to ask himself whether this move, no matter how well-intentioned, is legal, ethical, and moral. Jorge, while not happy about it, walks away from hiring Brewster.

Beth invites Jorge to lunch to talk out any bruised feelings so that their relationship remains robust. She needs to feel comfortable telling him things he doesn't necessarily want to hear. Jorge needs to foster a culture where Beth can and will tell him things he may not want to hear.

Learning

Jorge's knowledge of the biotech business outside of the recombinant DNA field is limited. Beth asks Karin, as Chief Medical Officer, to arrange a one-week road trip of biotechs that are more mature yet not in Acrux's niche. Beth arranges for a couple of retired biotech CEOs to join them for dinner to review the pitfalls of high-growth biotechs. Learn from history, learn from others!

Nine months ago, Acrux's largest customer received the wrong formulation of their flagship product. Jorge is furious and demands that heads roll. Beth asks him to step away until she completes the forensics. The investigation reveals cascading problems, many caused by rapid growth. Beth emphasizes to Jorge that this was a process problem, not a people problem. And she gently reminds him that he is ultimately responsible. Karin weighs in to keep Jorge's emotions in check. Beth and the team identify a detailed get-well program. Beth encourages

Jorge to acknowledge his responsibility to the team, both in creating the problem and fixing it.

While Beth has a supersized role at Acrux, the buck stops on Jorge's desk.

Earlier this month, Jorge, Beth, Karin, and the marketing team brainstormed the rollout for the second wave of products. Jorge, who almost single-handedly created a scientific miracle with these next two products, wants to immediately and forcefully market them. No one else around the table is quite so sure; there are still multiple hurdles to clear. Jorge is insistent. Despite the stereotypical VC's instinct to go fast, the VC representative shares the caution. Jorge is still insistent.

Beth suggests a 15-minute break and invites Jorge to her office for a private discussion. Forcefully yet calmly, she lets Jorge know he needs to slow down. Having faced RPGs in Iraq, Beth is not afraid of telling Jorge "no." She shares a particularly poignant combat story that makes the point that bosses who ignore the collective wisdom of their subordinates put everyone in jeopardy. After a lively exchange, Jorge listens. He gets it.

Caring

Beth and Jorge need to look out for each other. Beth needs to periodically kick Jorge out of the lab so he can watch his kids grow up. Likewise, Jorge needs to insist that Beth and Jamir take long weekends totally disconnected from the phone and email.

Both have to insist on keeping it fresh for the other.

So, what would you do differently?

Take a look at the list of the 23 truths below, and ask yourself, "What else could Beth and Jorge do?"

Focusing
- If you don't know where you're going, any road will get you there.
- Make the main thing the main thing.
- What you see depends on where you stand.

Leading
- The buck stops here.
- Lead from the front.
- May the force be with you.

Actioning
- What are you going to do differently on Monday?
- Improvise, adapt, and overcome.
- Plans are nothing, planning is everything.
- It is better to sweat in peace than bleed in war.
- Why? Why? Why? Why? Why?

Philosophizing
- Do what you can, with what you've got, where you are at.
- Nothing hard is ever easy.
- What's the right thing to do here?
- Life is tough, but it's tougher if you're not smart.
- KISS
- Perpetual optimism is a force multiplier.
- Everything is connected to everything else.

Learning
- Those who do not learn from history are doomed to repeat it.
- Make mistakes. Learn from them. Move on.
- Listen.

Caring
- Leaders eat last.
- Life is short, eat dessert first!

SUMMARY AND AFTERWORD

The transformation from doer to manager to leader is a continuum, not a simple switch.

The process takes time, energy, and thought. And you need guides and guidelines.

Think back to the ancient navigators of the Pacific Ocean. To sail, in a glorified canoe with a sail, without the ability to replenish food or water, from Tahiti to Hawaii, without GPS, a compass, or even a sextant, was a dangerous and technically difficult undertaking.

The Polynesian mariners could sail to a tiny island in an empty sea by using the stars in the night sky and carefully observing the oceans and animal life.

Based on teaching by their elders, they knew that each destination island had a zenith star. So, if they lined up the heading of their tiny canoe on the zenith star, eventually, they would arrive at their target.

The 23 truths I've discussed are not the only wise sayings; there are as many maxims as there are stars in the sky. But by picking a critical few truths (*your* zenith stars) you too can navigate to those hard-to-reach spots.

There are many truths and anecdotes that you will use—the ones offered in this book are just a starting point.

I wrote this book to make a difference in the lives of those who have taken on the difficult and yet incredibly rewarding mantle of leadership.

Good luck and Godspeed.

ACKNOWLEDGMENTS

I want to start by first acknowledging my wife of 38 years, partner for 43 years, and friend of 47 years, Catherine Moore, MD. A practicing psychiatrist for more than a third of a century, she has taught me so much about myself and the human mind.

Many have contributed to the making of the book. I want to recognize the readers of the first draft: Lynelle Boamah, James and Carmen Beaubeaux, Jeff Fischbeck, Ashley Gambhir, and Beth Howell.

Many read subsequent drafts, but I want to express my thanks to Steve Bell, John Krause, Bob Durham, and Elizabeth Rafael.

My thanks to my mentor, Karla Olson, who guided me through getting this and the previous two manuscripts to print. The fabulous design team of Alan Dino Nebel and Ian Koviak at the Book-Designers made my words look great.

ABOUT THE AUTHOR

Tom Gehring was born in Cologne, Germany, in 1953 and lived in Germany, France, India, and the United States before graduating from Rice University with a double major in Electrical Engineering and Applied Mathematics in 1976.

He served for 22 years in the United States Navy, almost entirely at sea in nuclear submarines.

After retiring from active duty in 1998, he spent three years at Booz|Allen|Hamilton as a senior strategic consultant.

From 2001 until his retirement in 2015, he was the San Diego County Medical Society (SDCMS) CEO, representing more than 8,000 physicians in the eighth-largest city in the United States.

Since retiring, he has published two books, teaches, writes, and consults on leadership and management.

BIBLIOGRAPHY

7 Roles Great Leaders Don't Delegate, Tom Gehring

11 Questions Great Managers Ask & Answer, Tom Gehring

The 7 Habits of Highly Effective People, Stephen Covey

Leaders Eat Last, Simon Sinek

Scenarios: The Art of Strategic Conversation, Kees van der Heijden

Seeing Around Corners, Rita McGrath

Fire Your Excuses, Bill Dyment and Marcus Dayhoff

APPENDIX 1 - 23 TRUTHS

Focusing
- If you don't know where you're going, any road will get you there.
- Make the main thing the main thing.
- What you see depends on where you stand.

Leading
- The buck stops here.
- Lead from the front.
- May the force be with you.

Actioning
- What are you going to do differently on Monday?
- Plans are nothing, planning is everything.
- Improvise, adapt, and overcome.
- It is better to sweat in peace than bleed in war.
- Why? Why? Why? Why? Why? Why?

Philosophizing
- Do what you can, with what you've got, where you are at.
- Nothing hard is ever easy.
- What's the right thing to do here?
- Life is tough, but it's tougher if you're not smart.
- KISS
- Perpetual optimism is a force multiplier.
- Everything is connected to everything else.

Learning
- Those who do not learn from history are doomed to repeat it.
- Make mistakes. Learn from them. Move on.
- Listen.

Caring
- Leaders eat last.
- Life is short, eat dessert first!

APPENDIX 2 – THE KEYS TO TRANSFORMATION FOR ALL 23 TRUTHS

Each of the following items should be mentally preceded by

"As managers transform themselves into leaders, they..."

Section One – Focusing

If You Don't Know Where You're Going, Any Road Will Get You There
- Shift from dutifully executing the pathway (strategies or work plans) to thinking deeply about the start points and endpoints of the organizational journey.
- Do not blindly accept the current assessment of the present.
- Spend more and more time improving and refining their understanding of the present tense.
- Think more strategically and less tactically.
- Distinguish between tasks and strategies.
- Recognize that strategies do not a vision make.

Make the Main Thing the Main Thing
- Get away from trying to do it all.
- Pick the most important—the "main thing"—and ruthlessly prioritize it.
- Understand and differentiate multiple roles, and assign a "main thing" to each role.
- Accept and deal with shifting priorities that result in changes to the "main thing."

What You See Depends on Where You Stand
- Become much more deliberate about their physical or intellectual positioning.
- Deliberately expand the scope of their thinking by considering many more perspectives and options.
- Become more flexible on the level of detail they examine.
- Ignore neither the big picture nor the details, but learn to zoom from one to the other and everything in between.

Section Two – Leading

The Buck Stops Here
- Stop making excuses.
- Get to the bottom of problems, and understand the root cause(s).
- Stop shying away from responsibility, then accept responsibility, and finally, embrace responsibility.
- Think deeply about what could possibly go wrong and put up barriers to failure.
- Think deeply about what needs to go right and implement changes to make it so.
- When things go well, give credit to your team.
- When things go badly, accept the blame.

Lead from the Front
- Are more and more visible—physically, emotionally, reputationally, and intellectually—at the *front* of the organization.
- Continuously evaluate whether leading from the front is commensurate with the gain.
- Continuously evaluate whether their leadership positioning is creating positive or negative symbolism.
- Proactively look for opportunities to lead by example.

May the Force Be with You
- Know their power(s) and authority.
- Know the underlying reasons for those power(s) and authority.
- Thoughtfully break the rules when they have to.
- Use their power(s) and authority more effectively.
- Abuse their power(s) and authority less.

Section Three – Actioning

What Are You Going to Do Differently on Monday?
- Learn to accept uncertainty, bound risk, and then take action.
- Avoid studying problems to death.
- Accept that you will only have some fraction of the information to make a decision.
- Think like a manager and act like a leader.

Plans Are Nothing, Planning Is Everything
- Focus on plann*ing*, not plans.
- Question a plan's underlying assumptions.
- Probe low-probability/high-impact possibilities.
- Develop contingencies.
- Prioritize and resource options.
- Think through the actions to be taken if one of the "What ifs?" becomes real.

Improvise, Adapt, and Overcome
- Develop a questioning attitude that proactively examines what could possibly go wrong.
- Adopt the mental resilience to accept with a positive attitude that your well-laid-out plan is going to change.
- Embrace the maxim "Improvise, Adapt, Overcome" by encouraging creativity and innovation to arrive at novel solutions to new problems.

It Is Better to Sweat in Peace than Bleed in War
- Actively pursue insourcing training to their organization (and not the training department).
- Make the preparation as realistic as possible.
- Measure the effectiveness of training against real-world standards.

Why? Why? Why? Why? Why? Why?
- Develop a mindset of curiosity.
- Focus more and more on the underlying cause(s) rather than the symptoms.
- Resist the urge to accept facile answers that ignore common sense.
- Cultivate a sixth sense when something just doesn't feel right.
- Resist the urge to simply blame the obvious miscreant.

Section Four – Philosophizing

Do What You Can, with What You've Got, Where You Are At
- Become more accepting that they cannot change the entire world.
- Focus on changing that part of the world they influence.
- Expand their influence.

Nothing Hard Is Ever Easy
- Accept that difficulties are difficult.
- Appreciate that all the talent in the world is not going to magically change hard to easy.
- Keep their sense of humor.

APPENDIX 2 – THE KEYS TO TRANSFORMATION FOR ALL 23 TRUTHS

What's the Right Thing to Do Here?
- Know and live their values and ethics in the face of more and more difficult decisions.
- Are prepared to make choices where there are no winners.
- Are ready to make choices that trump the written and unwritten rules.
- Learn to tune in and trust their inner voices.

Life Is Tough, but It's Tougher If You're Not Smart
- Differentiate between those who want to do well (the great majority) and those who can't or won't.
- Once you determine those who can't or won't:
  - get rid of them, or
  - put them into a position where they can do no harm, or
  - train them, if possible.
- Differentiate between people mistakes and systems/process mistakes.
- Look much harder for systems/process mistakes.
- Make sure that the corrective action is not worse than the mistake.

KISS
- Keep it simple&short.

Perpetual Optimism Is a Force Multiplier
- Learn to be positive in the face of trouble.
- Don't lie or exaggerate.
- Keep their worry beads hidden.

Everything Is Connected to Everything Else
- Spot today's hidden connections.
- Peer into the future to spot the next connections.
- Learn to accept and thrive on political decisions—those made in the absence of, or contravention of, the facts.

Section Five – Learning

Those Who Do Not Learn from History Are Doomed to Repeat It
- Push the lessons-learned horizon farther back in history because history often repeats itself.
- Push the lessons-learned aperture wider by looking outside their industry.
- Aggressively share and record their lessons learned.

Make Mistakes. Learn from Them. Move On.
- Take risks, albeit calculated ones.
- Bound the risk: they make sure that if things don't work out as desired, the fallout is minimal and not career- or life-ending.
- Know that risk-taking is necessary for growth.

Listen
- Listen to themselves.
- Listen to those who don't think as they do.
- Listen to those who disagree with them.
- Listen for what didn't get said.
- Create a culture of speaking up.

Section Six – Caring

Leaders Eat Last
- Take care of all the needs of their people.
- Are genuine about that care.

Life Is Short, Eat Dessert First!
- Learn to take care of themselves first.
- Program "me time" into their daily schedule.
- Take the time to say nice things to themselves.
- Eat well, exercise, and get sleep.

APPENDIX 3 - WHAT ARE YOU GOING TO DO DIFFERENTLY ON MONDAY FOR ALL 23 TRUTHS

Focusing

If You Don't Know Where You're Going, Any Road Will Get You There

- Schedule a formal review of the current environment, vision, and strategies.
- Ask to see the work plan and the strategic plan, and:
    - ✓ Check that the work plan is detailed and site-specific.
    - ✓ Check that the strategic plan is high-level and applicable to everyone.
- Ask to see the metrics associated with the work plan, the strategic plan, and the outcomes associated with the vision.

Make the Main Thing the Main Thing

- Write down the "main thing" for each of your roles.
- Write down the "main thing" for each of your organizations.
- Create a written plan to reduce your distractions at work and at home.
- Schedule a formal review of priorities, including feedback on whether the "main thing" has enough resources.

What You See Depends on Where You Stand
- Examine the frame for one major upcoming decision, and assess whether you are looking at the decision too narrowly (or too broadly).
- Develop a list of new or different locations you will look at in the following months.

Leading

The Buck Stops Here
- Identify several recent failures and do a deep dive on causality.
- Put a sign on your desk that the buck stops here.
- Pick one current project where you can spread credit.
- For one future project, task your team to proactively search for potential problems.

Lead from the Front
- Find one opportunity in the next month to lead from the front.

May the Force Be with You
- Reflect on a past circumstance where you broke (or should have broken) a rule for the greater good.
- Write down at least three unwritten rules in your work world.

Actioning

What Are You Going to Do Differently on Monday?
- Ask what you're going to do differently.

Plans Are Nothing, Planning Is Everything
- Stress test the plan for one existing project to see whether the plan is robust enough to tolerate significant changes in circumstances.

- Examine the planning process for one future project to see whether low-probability but high-impact possibilities have been considered.

Improvise, Adapt, and Overcome
- For a project in process, re-look at what could go wrong.
- When, not if, a well-laid plan needs radical re-arrangement, encourage your team to "Improvise, Adapt, and Overcome."

It Is Better to Sweat in Peace than Bleed in War
- Initiate a complete review of your training program, including the training subjects, the training method, and the measurement of training effectiveness.
- Make it a point to attend several training sessions each month.

Why? Why? Why? Why? Why? Why?
- Probe deeper into a current problem or crisis to look for the bedrock of causality.
- After the next crisis, ask yourself, "How did I contribute to this problem, by either action or inaction?"

Philosophizing

Do What You Can, with What You've Got, Where You Are At
- Actively adopt a mindset of "Accepting gracefully and acting forcefully."
- Actively adopt a mindset of "You can't change the weather, but you can dress for it. And listen to the weather report."

Nothing Hard Is Ever Easy
- Change your perspective on one tough problem away from *moaning* about how hard it is, to *accepting* that it's tough.
- Share your perspective with your team, and encourage them to be realistic but not pessimistic.

What's the Right Thing to Do Here?
- At the next major difficult decision, ask out loud, "Is this the right thing to do?"
- At the next major difficult decision, ask out loud, "Is this (decision) moral, legal, and ethical?"

Life Is Tough, but It's Tougher If You're Not Smart
- Dig deeper into a recent error or mistake. Look for the process problem(s). Be less likely to blame just the people.
- With your senior leadership, identify those in your organization who fall into the 3 percent or 2 percent category, and develop a plan to minimize their harmful impact.

KISS
- Keep it simple&short.

Perpetual Optimism Is a Force Multiplier
- Pick a problem that worries or troubles you, and deliberately create a positive public perspective on it.

Everything Is Connected to Everything Else
- Pick a subset of your world and ask what the current and future unseen connections are or will be.

Learning

Those Who Do Not Learn from History Are Doomed to Repeat It
- Convene a study group to look at history and industries to identify several specific new ideas.
- Create a process for recording and sharing internal lessons learned.

Make Mistakes. Learn from Them. Move On.
- Pick an event or evolution where you will encourage and tolerate risk-taking and mistakes.

APPENDIX 3 – WHAT ARE YOU GOING TO DO DIFFERENTLY

Listen

- Create a "kitchen cabinet" of trusted peers who are willing and able to tell you the uncomfortable truths.
- Set up a process where you proactively seek out team members to tell you the uncomfortable truths.

Caring

Leaders Eat Last

- For a current project, find out whether your people have what they need to do the work you assigned.

Life Is Short, Eat Dessert First!

- Find something nice to say to yourself about something great you did this week.
- Fence at least 30 minutes at work every day that only your spouse or significant other may interrupt.

APPENDIX 4 – ONE CEO'S PHILOSOPHY STATEMENT – PRETTY GOOD RULES TO LIVE BY

Below is a verbatim transcript of the philosophy statement that hung over my desk during my time as CEO. It was a living document that I periodically revised and reissued. Every member of my team had the document, as did my bosses. Since I plagiarized shamelessly to create this document, please do not hesitate to use it for whatever helps you become a better leader.

Eagle-eyed proofreaders among you will notice there is a typo: "monthly" is *deliberately* misspelled. I wanted to quickly teach my team that I was not infallible and that I expected—demanded—that they would correct me when I was wrong.

So if, after first reading it, they did not come back to me with a correction, I used that as a teachable moment:

- ✓ for better proofreading, if they didn't catch the mistake, and
- ✓ for the expectation that they correct me when I failed to live up to my own philosophy.

I'm a hard charger and a pragmatist—I expect you to be the same.

The physicians define a job well done.
- We exist, as an organization and as employees, to serve our member Physicians.
- Anticipate and deliver what Physician members of SDCMS consider value.
- If SDCMS does not satisfy the requirements of Physician members, someone else will.

Process, Output, and Outcome
- Use a process-driven approach to problem-solving.
- Document, understand, and improve your processes.
- Initiate planned abandonment regularly.
- Hate bureaucracy—challenge rules or processes that slow execution or fail to add value.

Communicating
- "I don't know" is an acceptable answer.
- If you don't understand, ask.
- If you're mad at me, or when (not if) I'm wrong, tell me.
- Keep the written and spoken word short and to the point.
- When we talk, give me the short version first. Insist on giving me the long version if you feel it necessary.
- When you write, use the format "Facts, Discussion, Action."
  - Facts = what do you know.
  - Discussion = what do you think.
  - Action = what do you want (me) to do.
- When you give a presentation, answer the following questions for the person receiving the brief:
  - What do you want them to do?
  - Why do you want them to do that?
  - What's in it for them?
  - How much does it cost, and how long will it take?
- Always feel free to call me—anytime, anywhere, for any reason. If in doubt about calling, call. If in doubt about being in doubt, call.

APPENDIX 4 - ONE CEO'S PHILOSOPHY STATEMENT

Mistakes & Risk
- Take risks—but understand the risk, bound the risk, and keep me cut in.
- I do not tolerate unmitigated risks, errors, or omissions on items identified as "Mission Critical."
- Mistakes happen—tell me about them.
- Identify and fix the root cause of mistakes.

Honesty
- Tell the truth—always—above all, to yourself.
- Do the right thing. If it feels wrong, it probably is.
- There are no secrets.[74]
- Keep your promises.
- I expect candor—if "the emperor has no clothes," say so.

Assignments
- If I want you to drop everything, I will tell you.
- Discuss our collective focus/issues/agendas/approach prior to proceeding.
- Keep me posted. Let me know when you will complete assignments and stick to your deadlines.
- Keep a list of your pending work for me.
- Keep a PUBLIC list of your top 10 focus points. Share them with me montlhy.
- Know your focus. Keep the focus in focus.

Interactions
- When communicating with other organizations, the word "No" belongs to me unless the request is illegal, unethical, or immoral.
- Never get into an argument (as opposed to a discussion) with a physician or an organization unless I know about it.
- If anyone behaves inappropriately with you, tell me immediately.

---

[74] Except salaries and personnel actions

Feedback
- We will meet for at least one hour every quarter to talk about us. Please take responsibility for making that happen.
- I will provide you written feedback annually. I will ask the staff to do likewise for me.

Meetings
- I hate long meetings.
- Meetings will start and end on time. If you must be late, please let me know ahead of time.
- If you are not ready for a meeting, reschedule the meeting and get ready.
- Send me a post-meeting email on all commitments made.

Network
- We are a network, not a hierarchy.
- Communicate, communicate, communicate, and communicate again.
- Serve each other's needs—we are a team.

Technology
- I want us to be on the cutting edge of new technology as soon as possible.
- Technology is a servant, not a master.

Passion
- See change as opportunity, not threat.
- Believe you can change the world.
- If in doubt, the glass is half-full!

INDEX

A
accepting and acting, 91–95
Ackerman, Gary, 45
actioning
    in case studies, 160–61, 168, 177
    changes and, 57–62
    importance of, 3, 55
    improvising and, 71–76
    planning and, 63–69
    training and, 77–81
    truths for, 3, 55
    understanding problems and, 83–88
adapting, 71–76
adversity, facing, 97–100
assumptions, questioning, 64–65
attitude, changing, 73–74

B
Beaubeaux, Jim, 60
Berra, Yogi, 130
Black Swan exercise, 65–67
Brown, C. Q., 58
Buchheim, Lothar-Günther, 118

C
caring
    in case studies, 163, 169–70, 179
    importance of, 4, 143
    leadership and, 145–47
    self-care, 149–53
    truths for, 4, 143
Carroll, Lewis, 13
case studies
    #1: transitioning from manager to leader, 157–64

#2: transitioning from doer to manager and leader, 165–71
#3: transitioning straight from doer to leader, 173–80
The CEO's Philosophy, 102, 203–6
Challenger space shuttle explosion, 138–39
Clemins, Archie, 99
The Confession, 101
connections, seeing, 121–26
contingencies, 67–68
Copenhagen, Battle of, 68
Corcoran, Corky, 97, 98
Covey, Stephen, 21, 91
COVID pandemic, 45, 104
credit, giving, 39–40, 46

D
Das Boot, 118
Dayhoff, Marcus, 58
decision making, 57–62, 101–7, 122
delegating, 16–17
Dilbert, 22, 86
Disney, 131
distractions, ignoring, 25
doing
    definition of, 1
    as stage in professional trajectory, 1
Drucker, Peter, 139
Dyment, Bill, 58

E
Eastwood, Clint, 71
Einstein, Albert, 29
Eisenhower, Dwight D., 63
The Empire Strikes Back, 49
environment, assessment of, 15–16
ethics, 101–7
Etter, Tom, 26
excuses, making, 38

F
Fitzgerald, F. Scott, 60
focusing
    in case studies, 158–59, 166–67, 175–76
    importance of, 3, 11
    on the main thing, 21–28
    perspective and, 29–33
    truths for, 3, 11–12
    vision and, 13–19
The Friends of Eddie Coyle, 109
future, visualizing, 16

G
Gates, Bill, 129
George II, King, 43
The Golden Rule, 102
Google, 130
Great Recession, 45
groupthink, 138–39

H
Haddo, USS, 27, 51, 97–99
Heartbreak Ridge, 71
Hemp, Paul, 32
history, repeating vs. learning from, 65, 129–32
Homer, 25
honesty, 97–100
Horace, 149
humor, sense of, 99

I
improvising, 71–76

K
Karr, Jean-Baptiste Alphonse, 130
Kelly, Walt, 86
Kingsley, Ben, 101, 102

L
leading
    caring and, 145–47

INDEX

in case studies, 159-60, 167-68, 176-77
credit and, 39-40
definition of, 1
from the front, 43-47
importance of, 3
perspective and, 31-32
planning and, 64
power and, 49-54
responsibility and, 37-41
self-care and, 149-53
as stage in professional trajectory, 1
symbolism and, 45-46, 145
transitioning from managing to, 2, 10, 35, 46, 181
truths for, 3, 35
learning
in case studies, 162, 169, 178-79
from history, 65, 129-32
importance of, 4, 127
from listening, 137-41
from mistakes, 133-36
from success, 135
truths for, 4, 127-28
Leonardo da Vinci, 121
Lewis, C. S., 29
Lincoln, Abraham, 99
listening, 137-41

M

managing
definition of, 1
multiple roles and, 23-24, 25-26
perspective and, 31-32
planning and, 64
power and, 50
responsibility and, 39
as stage in professional trajectory, 1

transitioning to leading from, 2, 10, 35, 46, 181
Marx, Karl, 130
McGrath, Rita, 124
McKee, USS, 26
Medical Injury Compensation Reform Act (MICRA), 122
Microsoft, 129-30
mistakes
causes of, 109-13
learning from, 133-36
moving on from, 135
Monday, symbolism of, 57, 61

N

Nautilus, USS, 44-45, 98, 134
Nelson, Horatio, 68
Niebuhr, Reinhold, 92

O

optimism, perpetual, 117-20

P

Pearl Harbor attack, 64-65, 135
perspective, 29-33
Petraeus, David, 52, 133
philosophizing
accepting and acting, 91-95
in case studies, 161-62, 168, 177-78
doing the right thing, 101-7
facing adversity, 97-100
importance of, 4, 89
perpetual optimism, 117-20
preventing and mitigating stupidity, 109-13
seeing connections, 121-26
simplicity, 115
truths for, 4, 90
philosophy statement, as CEO, 102, 203-6
planning, 15, 18, 55, 63-69. *See also* improvising

Pogo, 86
Pogy, USS, 30, 59, 67, 72-73, 74, 99, 131
political decisions, 122
Port Arthur attack, 64
positioning
    conceptual, 31
    physical, 30-31
positivity, 117-20
Powell, Colin, 117
power, 49-54
preparation
    active vs. passive, 78-79
    importance of, 77-78
    realism and, 79-80
priorities
    setting, 22-26
    shifting, 27
problems, determining root cause of, 83-88
professional life, four stages of, 1-2
Proposition 46, 122-23

Q

questions
    asking, 73
    about assumptions, 64-65
    "What if?" 65-67

R

Reagan, Ronald, 39
resilience, mental, 74
responsibility
    accepting, 39
    embracing, 37-41
    total, 37-38
Rickover, Hyman, 51-52, 83, 98
right thing, doing, 101-7
risk taking, 44, 133, 134
Roberts, Ron, 46
Roosevelt, Theodore, 90, 91, 92, 93, 130
Royal Dutch Shell, 66
rule of 95/3/2, 110-11
rules
    breaking, 51-52
    ethics conflicting with, 103-4

S

San Diego County Medical Society (SDCMS), 50, 60, 79-80, 105, 124, 139
The Sands of Iwo Jima, 109
Santayana, George, 129
scenario planning, 66
Schwarzkopf, Norman, 77, 101, 102
self-care, 149-53
Semper Gumby, 74
sensing, 14
The Serenity Prayer, 92
Sharer, Kevin, 32
Sharp HealthCare, 130-31
simplicity, power of, 115
Sinek, Simon, 145
Sophie's Choice, 104
Star Wars, 49
Stewart, Frank, 150
strategic planning, 15, 18, 55
stupidity, preventing and mitigating, 109-13
success, learning from, 135

T

Taleb, Nassim Nicholas, 65
teaching
    definition of, 2
    as stage in professional trajectory, 2
Thresher, USS, 52
Torres, Jacques, 149
training, 77-81
Truman, Harry, 37, 39
truth telling, 97, 99
Tsushima, Battle of, 135

23 truths
    alternative labels for, 5
    categorization of, 2-4
    characteristics of, 6
    keys to transformation for, 191-96
    list of, 188-89
    personalizing, 7, 181
    significance of number of, 6
    things to do differently on Monday for, 197-201

V

vacations, 150, 152
van der Heijden, Kees, 66
vision
    importance of, 13-19
    lack of, 14
    strategic planning and, 15, 18
von Moltke, Helmut, 72

W

Wayne, John, 109
"What if?" questions, 65-67
Widener, Bill, 91
wishful thinking, 118

Made in the USA
Las Vegas, NV
17 January 2024